Online Resources

Included with your purchase are multiple online resources. This includes the practice tests in an interactive format and a convenient study timer to help you manage your time.

Instructions for accessing these resources can be found on the last page of this book.

SSAT® Elementary Level Prep Book 2025-2026

3 Practice Tests and SSAT Study Guide for Grades 3 and 4
[Includes Detailed Answer Explanations]

Lydia Morrison

Copyright © 2025 by TPB Publishing

All rights reserved. No part of this publication may be reproduced, distributed, or transmitted in any form or by any means, including photocopying, recording, or other electronic or mechanical methods, without the prior written permission of the publisher, except in the case of brief quotations embodied in critical reviews and certain other noncommercial uses permitted by copyright law.

Written and edited by TPB Publishing.

TPB Publishing is not associated with or endorsed by any official testing organization. TPB Publishing is a publisher of unofficial educational products. All test and organization names are trademarks of their respective owners. Content in this book is included for utilitarian purposes only and does not constitute an endorsement by TPB Publishing of any particular point of view.

ISBN 13: 9781637751947

Table of Contents

Welcome ---- 1

Quick Overview ---- 2

Test-Taking Strategies ---- 3

Introduction to the SSAT Elementary Test ---- 7

Study Prep Plan for the SSAT Elementary Test ---- 9

Quantitative Section ---- *13*

   Practice Quiz ---- 33

   Answer Explanations ---- 35

Verbal Section ---- *36*

   Practice Quiz ---- 44

   Answer Explanations ---- 45

Reading Section ---- *46*

   Practice Quiz ---- 55

   Answer Explanations ---- 57

Writing Sample ---- *58*

Practice Writing Sample ---- *61*

SSAT Elementary Practice Test #1 ---- *65*

   Quantitative Section ---- 65

   Verbal Section ---- 71

   Reading Section ---- 75

   Writing Sample ---- 83

Answer Explanations ---- *87*

   Quantitative Section ---- 87

Verbal Section 90

Reading Section 93

SSAT Elementary Practice Test #2 97

Quantitative Section 97

Verbal Section 104

Reading Section 109

Writing Sample 116

Answer Explanations 120

Quantitative Section 120

Verbal Section 123

Reading Section 126

SSAT Elementary Practice Test 3 130

Quantitative Section 130

Verbal Section 137

Reading Section 142

Writing Sample 149

Answer Explanations 154

Quantitative Section 154

Verbal Section 157

Reading Section 161

Online Resources 166

Welcome

Dear Reader,

Welcome to your new Test Prep Books study guide! We are pleased that you chose us to help you prepare for your exam. There are many study options to choose from, and we appreciate you choosing us. Studying can be a daunting task, but we have designed a smart, effective study guide to help prepare you for what lies ahead.

Whether you're a parent helping your child learn and grow, a high school student working hard to get into your dream college, or a nursing student studying for a complex exam, we want to help give you the tools you need to succeed. We hope this study guide gives you the skills and the confidence to thrive, and we can't thank you enough for allowing us to be part of your journey.

In an effort to continue to improve our products, we welcome feedback from our customers. We look forward to hearing from you. Suggestions, success stories, and criticisms can all be communicated by emailing us at support@testprepbooks.com.

Sincerely,

Test Prep Books Team

Quick Overview

As you draw closer to taking your exam, effective preparation becomes more and more important. Thankfully, you have this study guide to help you get ready. Use this guide to help keep your studying on track and refer to it often.

This study guide contains several key sections that will help you be successful on your exam. The guide contains tips for what you should do the night before and the day of the test. Also included are test-taking tips. Knowing the right information is not always enough. Many well-prepared test takers struggle with exams. These tips will help equip you to accurately read, assess, and answer test questions.

A large part of the guide is devoted to showing you what content to expect on the exam and to helping you better understand that content. In this guide are practice test questions so that you can see how well you have grasped the content. Then, answer explanations are provided so that you can understand why you missed certain questions.

Don't try to cram the night before you take your exam. This is not a wise strategy for a few reasons. First, your retention of the information will be low. Your time would be better used by reviewing information you already know rather than trying to learn a lot of new information. Second, you will likely become stressed as you try to gain a large amount of knowledge in a short amount of time. Third, you will be depriving yourself of sleep. So be sure to go to bed at a reasonable time the night before. Being well-rested helps you focus and remain calm.

Be sure to eat a substantial breakfast the morning of the exam. If you are taking the exam in the afternoon, be sure to have a good lunch as well. Being hungry is distracting and can make it difficult to focus. You have hopefully spent lots of time preparing for the exam. Don't let an empty stomach get in the way of success!

When travelling to the testing center, leave earlier than needed. That way, you have a buffer in case you experience any delays. This will help you remain calm and will keep you from missing your appointment time at the testing center.

Be sure to pace yourself during the exam. Don't try to rush through the exam. There is no need to risk performing poorly on the exam just so you can leave the testing center early. Allow yourself to use all of the allotted time if needed.

Remain positive while taking the exam even if you feel like you are performing poorly. Thinking about the content you should have mastered will not help you perform better on the exam.

Once the exam is complete, take some time to relax. Even if you feel that you need to take the exam again, you will be well served by some down time before you begin studying again. It's often easier to convince yourself to study if you know that it will come with a reward!

Test-Taking Strategies

1. Predicting the Answer

When you feel confident in your preparation for a multiple-choice test, try predicting the answer before reading the answer choices. This is especially useful on questions that test objective factual knowledge. By predicting the answer before reading the available choices, you eliminate the possibility that you will be distracted or led astray by an incorrect answer choice. You will feel more confident in your selection if you read the question, predict the answer, and then find your prediction among the answer choices. After using this strategy, be sure to still read all of the answer choices carefully and completely. If you feel unprepared, you should not attempt to predict the answers. This would be a waste of time and an opportunity for your mind to wander in the wrong direction.

2. Reading the Whole Question

Too often, test takers scan a multiple-choice question, recognize a few familiar words, and immediately jump to the answer choices. Test authors are aware of this common impatience, and they will sometimes prey upon it. For instance, a test author might subtly turn the question into a negative, or he or she might redirect the focus of the question right at the end. The only way to avoid falling into these traps is to read the entirety of the question carefully before reading the answer choices.

3. Looking for Wrong Answers

Long and complicated multiple-choice questions can be intimidating. One way to simplify a difficult multiple-choice question is to eliminate all of the answer choices that are clearly wrong. In most sets of answers, there will be at least one selection that can be dismissed right away. If the test is administered on paper, the test taker could draw a line through it to indicate that it may be ignored; otherwise, the test taker will have to perform this operation mentally or on scratch paper. In either case, once the obviously incorrect answers have been eliminated, the remaining choices may be considered. Sometimes identifying the clearly wrong answers will give the test taker some information about the correct answer. For instance, if one of the remaining answer choices is a direct opposite of one of the eliminated answer choices, it may well be the correct answer. The opposite of obviously wrong is obviously right! Of course, this is not always the case. Some answers are obviously incorrect simply because they are irrelevant to the question being asked. Still, identifying and eliminating some incorrect answer choices is a good way to simplify a multiple-choice question.

4. Don't Overanalyze

Anxious test takers often overanalyze questions. When you are nervous, your brain will often run wild, causing you to make associations and discover clues that don't actually exist. If you feel that this may be a problem for you, do whatever you can to slow down during the test. Try taking a deep breath or counting to ten. As you read and consider the question, restrict yourself to the particular words used by the author. Avoid thought tangents about what the author *really* meant, or what he or she was *trying* to say. The only things that matter on a multiple-choice test are the words that are actually in the question. You must avoid reading too much into a multiple-choice question, or supposing that the writer meant something other than what he or she wrote.

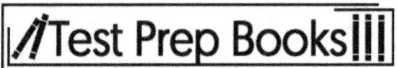

5. No Need for Panic

It is wise to learn as many strategies as possible before taking a multiple-choice test, but it is likely that you will come across a few questions for which you simply don't know the answer. In this situation, avoid panicking. Because most multiple-choice tests include dozens of questions, the relative value of a single wrong answer is small. As much as possible, you should compartmentalize each question on a multiple-choice test. In other words, you should not allow your feelings about one question to affect your success on the others. When you find a question that you either don't understand or don't know how to answer, just take a deep breath and do your best. Read the entire question slowly and carefully. Try rephrasing the question a couple of different ways. Then, read all of the answer choices carefully. After eliminating obviously wrong answers, make a selection and move on to the next question.

6. Confusing Answer Choices

When working on a difficult multiple-choice question, there may be a tendency to focus on the answer choices that are the easiest to understand. Many people, whether consciously or not, gravitate to the answer choices that require the least concentration, knowledge, and memory. This is a mistake. When you come across an answer choice that is confusing, you should give it extra attention. A question might be confusing because you do not know the subject matter to which it refers. If this is the case, don't

eliminate the answer before you have affirmatively settled on another. When you come across an answer choice of this type, set it aside as you look at the remaining choices. If you can confidently assert that one of the other choices is correct, you can leave the confusing answer aside. Otherwise, you will need to take a moment to try to better understand the confusing answer choice. Rephrasing is one way to tease out the sense of a confusing answer choice.

7. Your First Instinct

Many people struggle with multiple-choice tests because they overthink the questions. If you have studied sufficiently for the test, you should be prepared to trust your first instinct once you have carefully and completely read the question and all of the answer choices. There is a great deal of research suggesting that the mind can come to the correct conclusion very quickly once it has obtained all of the relevant information. At times, it may seem to you as if your intuition is working faster even than your reasoning mind. This may in fact be true. The knowledge you obtain while studying may be retrieved from your subconscious before you have a chance to work out the associations that support it. Verify your instinct by working out the reasons that it should be trusted.

8. Key Words

Many test takers struggle with multiple-choice questions because they have poor reading comprehension skills. Quickly reading and understanding a multiple-choice question requires a mixture of skill and experience. To help with this, try jotting down a few key words and phrases on a piece of scrap paper. Doing this concentrates the process of reading and forces the mind to weigh the relative importance of the question's parts. In selecting words and phrases to write down, the test taker thinks about the question more deeply and carefully. This is especially true for multiple-choice questions that are preceded by a long prompt.

9. Subtle Negatives

One of the oldest tricks in the multiple-choice test writer's book is to subtly reverse the meaning of a question with a word like *not* or *except*. If you are not paying attention to each word in the question, you can easily be led astray by this trick. For instance, a common question format is, "Which of the following is...?" Obviously, if the question instead is, "Which of the following is not...?," then the answer will be quite different. Even worse, the test makers are aware of the potential for this mistake and will include one answer choice that would be correct if the question were not negated or reversed. A test taker who misses the reversal will find what he or she believes to be a correct answer and will be so confident that he or she will fail to reread the question and discover the original error. The only way to avoid this is to practice a wide variety of multiple-choice questions and to pay close attention to each and every word.

10. Reading Every Answer Choice

It may seem obvious, but you should always read every one of the answer choices! Too many test takers fall into the habit of scanning the question and assuming that they understand the question because they recognize a few key words. From there, they pick the first answer choice that answers the question they believe they have read. Test takers who read all of the answer choices might discover that one of the latter answer choices is actually *more* correct. Moreover, reading all of the answer choices can remind you of facts related to the question that can help you arrive at the correct answer. Sometimes, a misstatement or incorrect detail in one of the latter answer choices will trigger your memory of the subject and will enable you to find the right answer. Failing to read all of the answer choices is like not reading all of the items on a restaurant menu: you might miss out on the perfect choice.

11. Spot the Hedges

One of the keys to success on multiple-choice tests is paying close attention to every word. This is never truer than with words like *almost*, *most*, *some*, and *sometimes*. These words are called "hedges" because they indicate that a statement is not totally true or not true in every place and time. An absolute statement will contain no hedges, but in many subjects, the answers are not always straightforward or absolute. There are always exceptions to the rules in these subjects. For this reason,

you should favor those multiple-choice questions that contain hedging language. The presence of qualifying words indicates that the author is taking special care with his or her words, which is certainly important when composing the right answer. After all, there are many ways to be wrong, but there is only one way to be right! For this reason, it is wise to avoid answers that are absolute when taking a multiple-choice test. An absolute answer is one that says things are either all one way or all another. They often include words like *every*, *always*, *best*, and *never*. If you are taking a multiple-choice test in a subject that doesn't lend itself to absolute answers, be on your guard if you see any of these words.

12. Long Answers

In many subject areas, the answers are not simple. As already mentioned, the right answer often requires hedges. Another common feature of the answers to a complex or subjective question are qualifying clauses, which are groups of words that subtly modify the meaning of the sentence. If the question or answer choice describes a rule to which there are exceptions or the subject matter is complicated, ambiguous, or confusing, the correct answer will require many words in order to be expressed clearly and accurately. In essence, you should not be deterred by answer choices that seem excessively long. Oftentimes, the author of the text will not be able to write the correct answer without offering some qualifications and modifications. Your job is to read the answer choices thoroughly and completely and to select the one that most accurately and precisely answers the question.

13. Restating to Understand

Sometimes, a question on a multiple-choice test is difficult not because of what it asks but because of how it is written. If this is the case, restate the question or answer choice in different words. This process serves a couple of important purposes. First, it forces you to concentrate on the core of the question. In order to rephrase the question accurately, you have to understand it well. Rephrasing the question will concentrate your mind on the key words and ideas. Second, it will present the information to your mind in a fresh way. This process may trigger your memory and render some useful scrap of information picked up while studying.

14. True Statements

Sometimes an answer choice will be true in itself, but it does not answer the question. This is one of the main reasons why it is essential to read the question carefully and completely before proceeding to the answer choices. Too often, test takers skip ahead to the answer choices and look for true statements. Having found one of these, they are content to select it without reference to the question above. The savvy test taker will always read the entire question before turning to the answer choices. Then, having settled on a correct answer choice, he or she will refer to the original question and ensure that the selected answer is relevant. The mistake of choosing a correct-but-irrelevant answer choice is especially common on questions related to specific pieces of objective knowledge.

15. No Patterns

One of the more dangerous ideas that circulates about multiple-choice tests is that the correct answers tend to fall into patterns. These erroneous ideas range from a belief that B and C are the most common right answers, to the idea that an unprepared test-taker should answer "A-B-A-C-A-D-A-B-A." It cannot be emphasized enough that pattern-seeking of this type is exactly the WRONG way to approach a multiple-choice test. To begin with, it is highly unlikely that the test maker will plot the correct answers according to some predetermined pattern. The questions are scrambled and delivered in a random order. Furthermore, even if the test maker was following a pattern in the assignation of correct answers, there is no reason why the test taker would know which pattern he or she was using. Any attempt to discern a pattern in the answer choices is a waste of time and a distraction from the real work of taking the test. A test taker would be much better served by extra preparation before the test than by reliance on a pattern in the answers.

Introduction to the SSAT Elementary Test

Function of the Test

The Secondary School Admission Test (SSAT) is a standardized test used for students applying to an independent or private school to determine if students have the necessary skills for success in a college preparatory program. The elementary level SSAT assesses basic math, verbal, reading, and writing skills in 3rd and 4th grade students who are applying to 4th and 5th grade. The test is administered nationwide in the US and is available in several other countries. The standard SSAT is administered on specific dates throughout the year. While middle and upper level SSATs allow for a Flex test administered on different dates, the Flex test is not available at the elementary level.

Test Administration

The standard SSAT is offered on six Saturdays throughout the year, with the elementary-level tests beginning in December. The test is available at hundreds of testing centers in the US and locations throughout the world. Students may only take the Flex SSAT once in an academic year, but can repeat the standard SSAT on any of the designated dates throughout the year. Elementary level students may only take the test twice in an academic year.

Closed Standard Test
If you are testing with a member school that is not open to the public, you will take a "closed" Standard test, which requires an access code obtained directly from the school for registration.

Open Standard Test
An open Standard test is an administration that is open to the general public. No access code is required for an Open Standard test.

Limited Standard Test
Sunday testing is available to those who observe religious events on Saturdays, but must be approved before registration.

The SSAT Flex Test
A Flex test is an in-person paper exam that can be taken any day except when the Standard test is administered. The Flex test may be provided in an open or closed format. Same as the Standard test, Open Flex tests are open to the general public and do not require an access code. The Closed Flex test requires an access code.

Students may repeat the standard test without penalty. Students must create an account on the SSAT website in order to register. This account also allows students to print their admission tickets and receive their test scores. Registration opens about 10 weeks prior to a testing date. Late registration begins 3 weeks before the test date and rush registration starts 10 days before the test date. Late and rush registrations incur additional fees.

Testing accommodations are available for students with disabilities. Students requiring accommodations must apply and be approved before registering for the test. Approval is only required once in an academic year. The official guidelines for accommodations can be accessed on the SSAT.org website.

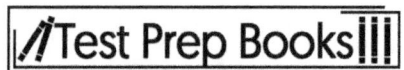

Introduction to the SSAT Elementary Test

Test Format

The elementary level SSAT is a four-part test consisting of multiple-choice questions in Quantitative (Math), Verbal, and Reading sections, and a writing sample. The writing sample is not scored. The Quantitative section includes 30 questions in the areas of addition, subtraction, multiplication, division, fractions, place value, and basic geometry and measurement. The Verbal section includes 30 questions in two categories: synonyms and analogies. The Reading section is divided into 7 passages, each with 4 questions, for a total of 28 questions. Questions focus mainly on reading comprehension, retention of information in the passage, and word meaning. The writing sample asks the student to write a response to a picture with a story that has a beginning, middle, and end.

Section	Questions	Question Type	Time Allotted
Quantitative	30	Multiple Choice	30 minutes
Verbal	30	Multiple Choice	20 minutes
Break			15 minutes
Reading	28	Multiple Choice	30 minutes
Writing Sample	1	Written Response	15 minutes
Experimental	15-17	Multiple Choice	15 minutes

Scoring

In the elementary level SSAT, there is no penalty for guessing. A free scoring report is available online through a student's SSAT account roughly 2 weeks after the test date. The report will include a narrative explanation of the scores, along with the number correct, percentage correct, a scaled score, percentile rank, and total scaled score. The possible scaled score ranges from 300 – 600. The percentile rank is from 1 – 99, and the total score is from 900 – 1800, with a mean of 1350. The SSAT is a norm-referenced test, meaning that the score is compared to a norm group of test takers' scores from the last 3 years. The score report will include the student's scores, as well as the average norm scores in each section for comparison. The percentile rank shows how a student did in comparison to the norm group. For example, if a student's percentile is 85, it means she scored the same or better than 85% of those in the norm group. The experimental section is used in testing content for future tests. A student's test will still be valid and scored with or without answering the experimental section.

Study Prep Plan for the SSAT Elementary Test

1 **Schedule** - Use one of our study schedules below or come up with one of your own.

2 **Relax** - Test anxiety can hurt even the best students. There are many ways to reduce stress. Find the one that works best for you.

3 **Execute** - Once you have a good plan in place, be sure to stick to it.

One Week Study Schedule

Day 1	Quantitative Section
Day 2	Verbal Section
Day 3	Writing Sample
Day 4	Practice Test #1
Day 5	Practice Test #2
Day 6	Practice Test 3
Day 7	Take Your Exam!

Two Week Study Schedule

Day 1	Quantitative Section	Day 8	Practice Test #1
Day 2	Place Value	Day 9	Answer Explanations
Day 3	Basic Concepts of Measurement	Day 10	Practice Test #2
Day 4	Verbal Section	Day 11	Answer Explanations
Day 5	Reading Section	Day 12	Practice Test 3
Day 6	Nonfiction Literature	Day 13	Answer Explanations
Day 7	Writing Sample	Day 14	Take Your Exam!

Build your own prep plan by visiting the Online Resources page.

Instructions and a QR code can be found on the last page of this guide.

As you study for your test, we'd like to take the opportunity to remind you that you are capable of great things! With the right tools and dedication, you truly can do anything you set your mind to. The fact that you are holding this book right now shows how committed you are. In case no one has told you lately, you've got this! Our intention behind including this coloring page is to give you the chance to take some time to engage your creative side when you need a little brain-break from studying. As a company, we want to encourage people like you to achieve their dreams by providing good quality study materials for the tests and certifications that improve careers and change lives. As individuals, many of us have taken such tests in our careers, and we know how challenging this process can be. While we can't come alongside you and cheer you on personally, we can offer you the space to recall your purpose, reconnect with your passion, and refresh your brain through an artistic practice. We wish you every success, and happy studying!

Quantitative Section

Basic Addition, Subtraction, Multiplication, and Division

Gaining more of something relates to addition, while taking something away relates to subtraction. Vocabulary words such as *total, more, less, left,* and *remain* are common when working with these problems. The + sign means plus. This shows that addition is happening. The − sign means minus. This shows that subtraction is happening. The symbols will be important when you write out equations.

Addition can also be defined in equation form. For example, $4 + 5 = 9$ shows that $4 + 5$ is the same as 9. Therefore, $9 = 9$, and "four plus five equals nine." When two quantities are being added together, the result is called the *sum*. Therefore, the sum of 4 and 5 is 9. The numbers being added, such as 4 and 5, are known as the *addends*.

Subtraction can also be in equation form. For example, $9 - 5 = 4$ shows that $9 - 5$ is the same as 4 and that "9 minus 5 is 4." The result of subtraction is known as a *difference*. The difference of $9 - 5$ is 4. 4 represents the amount that is left once the subtraction is done. The order in which subtraction is completed does matter. For example, $9 - 5$ and $5 - 9$ do not result in the same answer. $5 - 9$ results in a negative number. So, subtraction does not adhere to the commutative or associative property. The order in which subtraction is completed is important.

Multiplication is the addition of equal amounts. The answer to a multiplication problem is called a *product*. Products stand for the total number of items within different groups. The symbol for multiplication is × or ·. The equations 2×3 and $2 \cdot 3$ mean "2 times 3."

As an example, there are three sets of four apples. The goal is to know how many apples there are in total. Three sets of four apples gives $4 + 4 + 4 = 12$. Also, three times four apples gives $3 \times 4 = 12$. Therefore, for any whole numbers a and b, where a is not equal to zero, $a \times b = b + b + \cdots b$, where b is added a times. Also, $a \times b$ can be thought of as the number of units in a rectangular block consisting of a rows and b columns. For example, 3×7 is equal to the number of squares in the following rectangle:

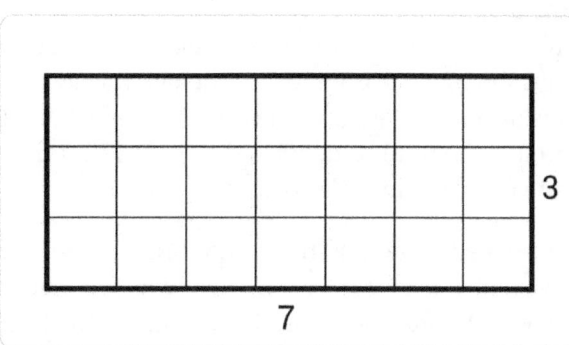

The answer is 21, and there are 21 squares in the rectangle.

With any number times one (for example, $8 \times 1 = 8$) the original amount does not change. Therefore, one is the *multiplicative identity*. For any whole number a, $1 \times a = a$. Also, any number multiplied times zero results in zero. Therefore, for any whole number a, $0 \times a = 0$.

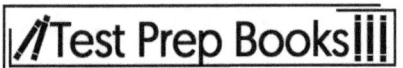

Quantitative Section

Division is based on dividing a given number into parts. For example, a pack of 20 pencils is to be divided amongst 10 children. Therefore, divide 20 by 10. In this example, each child would receive 2 pencils.

The symbol for division is ÷ or /. The equation above is written as $20 \div 10 = 2$, or $20 / 10 = 2$. This means "20 divided by 10 is equal to 2." Division can be explained as the following: for any whole numbers a and b, where b is not equal to zero, $a \div b = c$ if and only if $a = b \times c$. This means, division can be thought of as a multiplication problem with a missing part. For instance, calculating $20 \div 10$ is the same as asking the following: "If there are 20 items in total with 10 in each group, how many are in each group?" Therefore, 20 is equal to ten times what value? This question is the same as asking, "If there are 20 items in total split into 10 groups, how many are in each group?" Therefore, 20 is equal to 10 times an unknown value, which is 2.

In a division problem, a is known as the *dividend*, b is the *divisor*, and c is the *quotient*. Zero cannot be divided into parts. Therefore, for any nonzero whole number $a, 0 \div a = 0$. Also, division by zero is undefined. Dividing an amount into zero parts is not possible.

Harder division involves dividing a number into equal parts but having some left over. An example is dividing a pack of 20 pencils among 8 friends so that each friend receives the same number of pencils. In this setting, each friend receives 2 pencils. There are 4 pencils leftover. 20 is the dividend, 8 is the divisor, 2 is the quotient, and 4 is known as the *remainder*. Within this type of division problem, for whole numbers a, b, c, and d, $a \div b = c$ with a remainder of d. This is true if and only if:

$$a = (b \times c) + d$$

When calculating $a \div b$, if there is no remainder, a is said to be *divisible* by b. *Even numbers* are all divisible by the number 2. *Odd numbers* are not divisible by 2. An odd number of items cannot be paired up into groups of 2 without having one item leftover.

Addition and subtraction are "inverse operations." Adding a number and then subtracting the same number will cancel each other out. This results in the original number, and vice versa. For example, $8 + 7 - 7 = 8$ and $137 - 100 + 100 = 137$.

Multiplication and division are also inverse operations. So, multiplying by a number and then dividing by the same number results in the original number. For example, $8 \times 2 \div 2 = 8$ and $12 \div 4 \times 4 = 12$. Inverse operations are used to work backwards to solve problems. In the case that 7 and a number add to 18, the inverse operation of subtraction is used to find the unknown value ($18 - 7 = 11$). If a school's entire 4th grade was divided evenly into 3 classes each with 22 students, the inverse operation of multiplication is used to determine the total students in the grade ($22 \times 3 = 66$). More scenarios involving inverse operations are listed in the tables below.

Word problems take concepts learned in the classroom and turn them into real-life situations. Some parts of the problem are known and at least one part is unknown. There are three types of instances in which something can be unknown: the starting point, the change, or the final result. These can all be missing from the information given.

For an addition problem, the change is the quantity of a new amount added to the starting point.

For a subtraction problem, the change is the quantity taken away from the starting point.

Regarding addition, the given equation is $3 + 7 = 10$.

Quantitative Section

The number 3 is the starting point. 7 is the change, and 10 is the result from adding a new amount to the starting point. Different word problems can arise from this same equation, depending on which value is the unknown. For example, here are three problems:

- If a boy had 3 pencils and was given 7 more, how many would he have in total?
- If a boy had 3 pencils and a girl gave him more so that he had 10 in total, how many were given to him?
- A boy was given 7 pencils so that he had 10 in total. How many did he start with?

All three problems involve the same equation. Finding out which part of the equation is missing is the key to solving each word problem. The missing answers would be 10, 7, and 3.

In terms of subtraction, the same three scenarios can occur. The given equation is $6 - 4 = 2$.

The number 6 is the starting point. 4 is the change, and 2 is the new amount that is the result from taking away an amount from the starting point. Again, different types of word problems can arise from this equation. For example, here are three possible problems:

- If a girl had 6 quarters and 2 were taken away, how many would be left over?
- If a girl had 6 quarters, purchased a pencil, and had 2 quarters left over, how many did she pay with?
- If a girl paid for a pencil with 4 quarters and had 2 quarters left over, how many did she have to start with?

The three question types follow the structure of the addition word problems, and determining whether the starting point, the modification, or the final result is missing is the goal in solving the problem. The missing answers would be 2, 4, and 6, respectively.

The three addition problems and the three subtraction word problems can be solved by using a picture, a number line, or an algebraic equation. If an equation is used, a question mark can be utilized to represent the unknown quantity. For example, 6-2=? can be written to show that the missing value is the result. Using equation form visually indicates what portion of the addition or subtraction problem is the missing value.

Key words within a multiplication problem involve *times, product, doubled,* and *tripled.* Key words within a division problem involve *split, quotient, divided, shared, groups,* and *half.* Like addition and subtraction, multiplication and division problems also have three different types of missing values.

Multiplication

Multiplication consists of a certain number of groups, with the same amount of items within each group, and the total amount within all groups. Therefore, each one of these amounts can be the missing value.

For example, the given equation is $5 \times 3 = 15$.

5 and 3 are interchangeable, so either amount can be the number of groups or the number of items within each group. 15 is the total number of items. Again, different types of word problems can arise from this equation.

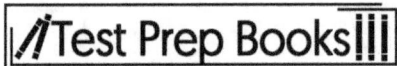

For example, here are three problems:

- If a classroom is serving 5 different types of apples for lunch and has 3 apples of each type, how many total apples are there to give to the students?
- If a classroom has 15 apples with 5 different types, how many of each type are there?
- If a classroom has 15 apples with 3 of each type, how many types are there to choose from?

Each question involves using the same equation to solve. It is important to decide which part of the equation is the missing value. The answers to the problems are 15, 3, and 5.

Division

Similar to multiplication, division problems involve a total amount, a number of groups having the same amount, and a number of items within each group. The difference between multiplication and division is that the starting point is the total amount. It then gets divided into equal amounts.

For example, the equation is $15 \div 5 = 3$.

15 is the total number of items, which is being divided into 5 different groups. In order to do so, 3 items go into each group. Also, 5 and 3 are interchangeable. So, the 15 items could be divided into 3 groups of 5 items each. Therefore, different types of word problems can arise from this equation. For example, here are three types of problems:

- A boy needs 48 pieces of chalk. If there are 8 pieces in each box, how many boxes should he buy?
- A boy has 48 pieces of chalk. If each box has 6 pieces in it, how many boxes did he buy?
- A boy has partitioned all of his chalk into 8 piles, with 6 pieces in each pile. How many pieces does he have in total?

Each one of these questions involves the same equation. The third question can easily utilize the multiplication equation $8 \times 6 = ?$ instead of division. The answers are 6, 8, and 48.

Another method of multiplication can be done with the use of an *area model*. An area model is a rectangle that is divided into rows and columns that match up to the number of place values within each number. Take the example 29×65. These two numbers can be split into simpler numbers: $29 = 25 + 4$ and $65 = 60 + 5$. The products of those 4 numbers are found within the rectangle and then summed up to get the answer. The entire process is:

$$(60 \times 25) + (5 \times 25) + (60 \times 4) + (5 \times 4) = 1{,}500 + 240 + 125 + 20 = 1{,}885$$

Quantitative Section

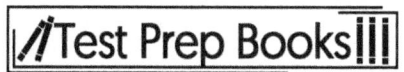

Here is the actual area model:

	25	4
60	60x25 1,500	60x4 240
5	5x25 125	5x4 20

```
  1,500
    240
    125
+    20
  1,885
```

Decimals and fractions are two ways to represent positive numbers less than one. Counting money in coins is a good way to visualize values less than one. This is because problems dealing with change are stories that are used in real life. For example, if a student had 3 quarters and a dime and wanted to purchase a cookie at lunch for 50 cents, how much change would she receive? The answer would be found by first calculating the sum of the change as 85 cents and then subtracting 50 cents to get 35 cents. Money can also be used as a way to understand the transition between decimals and fractions. For example, a dime represents $0.10 or $\frac{1}{10}$ of a dollar. Problems involving both dollars and cents should also be considered. For example, if someone has 3 dollar bills and 2 quarters, the amount can be represented as a decimal as $3.50.

Formally, a *decimal* is a number that has a dot in the number. For example, 3.45 is a decimal. The dot is called a *decimal point*. The number to the left of the decimal point is in the ones place. The number to the right of the decimal point represents the part of the number less than one. The first number to the right of the decimal point is the tenths place, and one tenth represents $\frac{1}{10}$, just like a dime. The next place is the hundredths place, and it represents $\frac{1}{100}$, just like a penny. This idea is continued to the right in the hundredths, thousandths, and ten thousandths places. Each place value to the right is ten times smaller than the one to its left.

A number less than one has only digits in some decimal places. For example, 0.53 is less than one. A *mixed number* is a number greater than one that also contains digits in some decimal places. For example, 3.43 is a mixed number. Adding a zero to the right of a decimal does not change the value of the number. For example, 2.75 is the same as 2.750. However, 2.75 is the more accepted representation of the number. Also, zeros are usually placed in the ones column in any value less than one. For example, 0.65 is the same as .65, but 0.65 is more widely used.

In order to read or write a decimal, the decimal point is ignored. The number is read as a whole number. Then the place value unit is stated where the last digit falls. For example, 0.089 is read as *eighty-nine thousandths*, and 0.1345 is read as *one thousand, three hundred forty-five ten thousandths*. In mixed

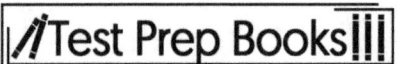

numbers, the word *and* is used to represent the decimal point. For example, 2.56 is read as *two and fifty-six hundredths*.

We multiply decimals the same way we multiply whole numbers. The only difference is that decimal places are included in the end result. For example, given the problem 87.5×0.45, the answer would be found by multiplying 875×45 to get 39,375. Then you would input a decimal point three places to the left because there are three total decimal places in the original problem. Therefore, the answer is 39.375.

Dividing a number by a single digit or two digits can be turned into repeated subtraction problems. An area model can be used throughout the problem that represents multiples of the divisor. For example, the answer to $8580 \div 55$ can be found by subtracting 55 from 8580 one at a time and counting the total number of subtractions necessary.

However, a simpler process involves using larger multiples of 55. First, $100 \times 55 = 5,500$ is subtracted from 8,580, and 3,080 is leftover. Next, $50 \times 55 = 2,750$ is subtracted from 3,080 to obtain 380. $5 \times 55 = 275$ is subtracted from 330 to obtain 55, and finally, $1 \times 55 = 55$ is subtracted from 55 to obtain zero. Therefore, there is no remainder, and the answer is $100 + 50 + 5 + 1 = 156$.

Here is a picture of the area model and the repeated subtraction process:

```
          55
100  | 5500           55 | 8580
 50  | 2750              -5500  (100 x 55)
  5  |  275              ─────
  1  |   55               3080
                         -2750  (50 x 55)
                         ─────
                          330
                         -275   (5 x 55)
                         ─────
                           55
                          -55   (1 x 55)
                         ─────
                            0
```

To check the answer of a division problem, multiply the answer times the divisor. This will help check to see if the dividend is obtained. If there is a remainder, the same process is done, but the remainder is added on at the end to try to match the dividend. In the previous example, $156 \times 55 = 8580$ would be the checking procedure. Dividing decimals involves the same repeated subtraction process. The only difference would be that the subtractions would involve numbers that include values in the decimal places. Lining up decimal places is crucial in this type of problem.

Order of Operations

When you're trying to solve a problem with more than one type of operation, there are certain steps to follow. These are called the order of operations. The different operations are parentheses, exponents, multiplication, division, addition, and subtraction. A common practice for remembering the order is the abbreviation "PEMDAS." This can be turned into "Please Excuse My Dear Aunt Sally". It should also be noted that multiplication and division are in the same rank and should be performed from left to right as they appear in the equation. The same goes for addition and subtraction. For example, solve the problem $8 - 2 \times 3 + 12 \div 4$. There are no parentheses or exponents in the problem. Therefore, we can go straight to the multiplication and division. After we multiply and divide, we are left with $8 - 6 + 3$. The addition and subtraction should be performed from left to right. This results in 5 as the answer.

Place Value

Numbers count in groups of 10. That number is the same throughout the set of natural numbers and whole numbers. It is referred to as working within a base 10 numeration system. Only the numbers from zero to 9 are used to represent any number. The foundation for doing this involves *place value*. Numbers are written side by side. This is to show the amount in each place value.

For place value, let's look at how the number 10 is different from zero to 9. It has two digits instead of just one. The one is in the tens' place, and the zero is in the ones' place. Therefore, there is one group of tens and zero ones. 11 has one 10 and one 1. The introduction of numbers from 11 to 19 should be the next step. Each value within this range of numbers consists of one group of 10 and a specific number of leftover ones. Counting by tens can be practiced once the tens column is understood. This process consists of increasing the number in the tens place by one. For example, counting by 10 starting at 17 would result in the next four values being 27, 37, 47, and 57.

A place value chart can be used for understanding and learning about numbers that have more digits. Here is an example of a place value chart:

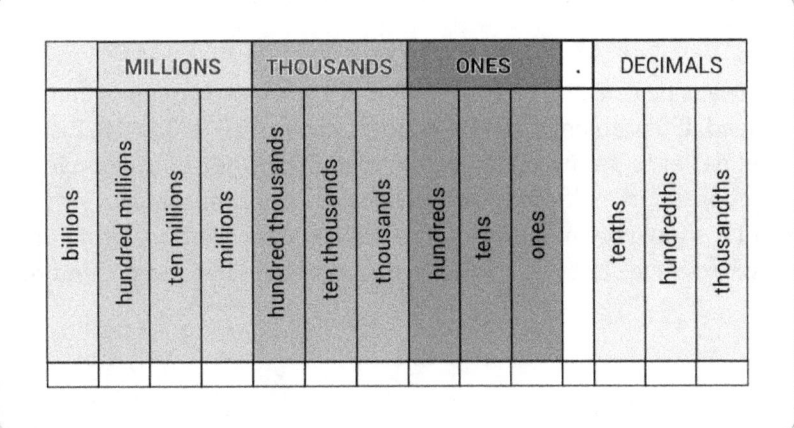

In the number 1,234, there are 4 ones and 3 tens. The 2 is in the hundreds' place, and the one is in the thousands' place. Note that each group of three digits is separated by a comma. The 2 has a value that is 10 times greater than the 3. Every place to the left has a value 10 times greater than the place to its right. Also, each group of three digits is also known as a *period*. 234 is in the ones' period.

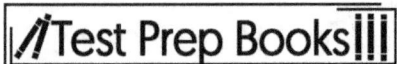

The number 1,234 can be written out as *one-thousand, two hundred thirty-four*. The process of writing out numbers is known as the *decimal system*. It is also based on groups of 10. The place value chart is a helpful tool in using this system. In order to write out a number, it always starts with the digit(s) in the highest period. For example, in the number 23,815,467, the 23 is in highest place and is in the millions' period. The number is read *twenty-three million, eight hundred fifteen thousand, four hundred sixty-seven*. Each period is written separately through the use of commas. Also, no "ands" are used within the number. Another way to think about the number 23,815,467 is through the use of an addition problem. For example:

$$23,815,467 = 20,000,000 + 3,000,000 + 800,000 + 10,000 + 5,000 + 400 + 60 + 7$$

This expression is known as *expanded form*. The actual number 23,815,467 is written in *standard form*.

Rounding is an important concept dealing with place value. *Rounding* is the process of either bumping a number up or down, based on a certain place value. First, the place value is specified. Then, the digit to its right is looked at. For example, if rounding to the nearest hundreds place, the digit in the tens place is used. If it is a zero, one, 2, 3, or 4, the digit being rounded to is left alone. If it is a 5, 6, 7, 8 or 9, the digit being rounded to is increased by one. All other digits before the decimal point are then changed to zeros, and the digits in decimal places are dropped. If a decimal place is being rounded to, all digits that come after are just dropped. For example, if 845,231.45 was to be rounded to the nearest thousands place, the answer would be 845,000. The 5 would remain the same due to the 2 in the hundreds place. Also, if 4.567 were to be rounded to the nearest tenths place, the answer would be 4.6. The 5 increased to 6 due to the 6 in the hundredths place, and the rest of the decimal is dropped.

In order to compare whole numbers with many digits, place value can be used. In each number to be compared, it is necessary to find the highest place value in which the numbers differ and to compare the value within that place value. For example, $4,523,345 < 4,532,456$ because of the values in the ten thousands place. A similar process can be used for decimals. However, number lines can also be used. Tick marks can be placed within two whole numbers on the number line that represent tenths, hundredths, etc. Each number being compared can then be plotted. The value farthest to the right on the number line is the largest.

Mental math should always be considered as problems are worked through. It can save time to work a problem out in your head. If a problem is simple enough, such as $15 + 3 = 18$, it should be completed in your head. It will get easier to do this once you know addition and subtraction in higher place values. Mental math is also important in multiplication and division. The times tables, for multiplying all numbers from one to 12, should be memorized. This will allow for division within those numbers to be memorized as well. For example, $121 \div 11 = 11$ because it should be memorized that $11 \times 11 = 121$.

Quantitative Section

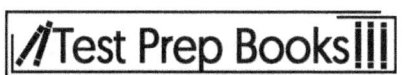

Here is the multiplication table to be memorized:

x	1	2	3	4	5	6	7	8	9	10	11	12	13	14	15
1	1	2	3	4	5	6	7	8	9	10	11	12	13	14	15
2	2	4	6	8	10	12	14	16	18	20	22	24	26	28	30
3	3	6	9	12	15	18	21	24	27	30	33	36	39	42	45
4	4	8	12	16	20	24	28	32	36	40	44	48	52	56	60
5	5	10	15	20	25	30	35	40	45	50	55	60	65	70	75
6	6	12	18	24	30	36	42	48	54	60	66	72	78	84	90
7	7	14	21	28	35	42	49	56	63	70	77	84	91	98	105
8	8	16	24	32	40	48	56	64	72	80	88	96	104	112	120
9	9	18	27	36	45	54	63	72	81	90	99	108	117	126	135
10	10	20	30	40	50	60	70	80	90	100	110	120	130	140	150
11	11	22	33	44	55	66	77	88	99	110	121	132	143	154	165
12	12	24	36	48	60	72	84	96	108	120	132	144	156	168	180
13	13	26	39	52	65	78	91	104	117	130	143	156	169	182	195
14	14	28	42	56	70	84	98	112	126	140	154	168	182	196	210
15	15	30	45	60	75	90	105	120	135	150	165	180	195	210	225

The values along the diagonal of the table consist of *perfect squares*. A perfect square is the product of two of the same numbers.

A *number line* is a visual representation of all real numbers. It is a straight line on which any number can be plotted. The origin is zero, and the values to the right of the origin represent positive numbers. Values to the left of the origin represent negative numbers. Both sides extend forever. Here is an example of a number line:

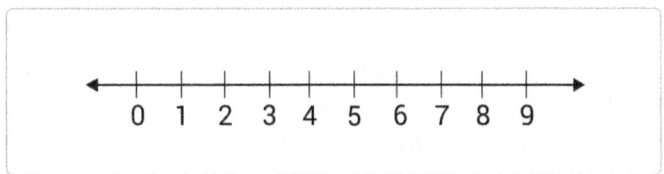

Number lines can be utilized for addition and subtraction. For example, it could be used to add $1 + 3$. Starting at one on the line, adding 3 to one means moving three units to the right to end up at 4. Therefore, $3 + 1$ is equal to 4. $5 - 2$ can also be determined. Start at 5 on the number line. Subtract 2 from 5. This means moving to the left two units from 5 to end up at 3. Therefore, $5 - 2$ is equal to 3.

The number line can also be used to show the additive and subtractive identity This is the rule that states when any integer is added to or subtracted from 0, it remains unchanged. What happens on the number line when you add or subtract zero? There is no movement along the line. For example, $5 + 0$ is equal to 5.

Addition adheres to the commutative property. This is because the order of the numbers being added does not matter. For example, both $4 + 5$ and $5 + 4$ equal 9. The *commutative property of addition* states that for any whole numbers a and b, it is true that $a + b = b + a$. Also, addition follows the

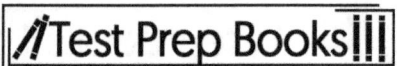

Quantitative Section

associative property because the sum of three or more numbers results in the same answer, no matter what order the numbers are in. Let's look at the following example. Remember that numbers inside parentheses are always calculated first: $1 + (2 + 3)$ and $(1 + 2) + 3$ both equal 6. *The associative property of addition* states that for any whole numbers a, b, and c, $(a + b) + c = a + (b + c)$.

Ordering of Numbers

In counting, when a number appears after another number in order, that number will be one more. On the other hand, when a number appears before another number in order, that number will be one less. This idea is useful when counting backward. Also, zero means that there is none of something. This idea can be seen by taking away all of something so that there are zero items left. Also, learning to count by tens starting at any number is a key concept. Once a new number is learned, learning how to read and write that number is also important.

Placing numbers in an order in which they are listed from smallest to largest is known as *ordering*. When items are listed by using numbers in order, the *ordinal numbers*, 1st, 2nd, 3rd, 4th, ..., can be used.

When you order numbers the right way, you can more easily compare the different amounts of items. When you compare numbers you show whether two amounts are the same or different. Teachers can show two different quantities of items in the classroom. Then they can discuss which amount is lesser or greater. This exercise also can be used in order to classify numbers from the smallest amount to the largest amount.

Being able to compare any two whole numbers without a visual representation is also an important task. Each whole number relates to a certain amount. This amount can be ranked and compared to other amounts. Knowing the right vocabulary relating to ordering and comparing is important. The *equals sign* is =. It shows that two numbers are the same on either side of the symbol. For example, $28 = 28$. The symbols that are used for comparison are < to represent *less than*, > to represent *greater than*. The symbols ≤ to represent *less than or equal to*, and ≥ to represent *greater than or equal to*, and ≠ to represent *not equal to* can also be used.

You can compare numbers with any number of digits when you use these symbols. For example, the expression $77 < 100$, should be understood as 77 is less than 100. The expression $44 > 23$ should be understood as 44 is greater than 23. The expression $22 \neq 24$ should be understood as 22 is not equal *to 24*. Also, both $36 = 36$ and $36 \leq 36$ can be written because both "36 equals 36" and "36 is less than or equal to 36" applies.

Patterns

Patterns are an important part of mathematics. When mathematical calculations are completed repeatedly, patterns can be recognized. Recognizing patterns is an integral part of mathematics because it helps you understand relationships between different ideas. For example, a sequence of numbers can be given, and being able to recognize the relationship between the given numbers can help in completing the sequence.

For instance, given the sequence of numbers 7, 14, 21, 28, 35, ..., the next number in the sequence would be 42. This is because the sequence lists all multiples of 7, starting at 7. Sequences can also be built from addition, subtraction, and division. Being able to recognize the relationship between the values that are given is the key to finding out the next number in the sequence.

Patterns within a sequence can come in two distinct forms. The items either repeat in a constant order, or the items change from one step to another in some consistent way. The core is the smallest unit, or number of items, that repeats in a repeating pattern. For example, the pattern ○○▲○○▲○... has a core that is ○○▲. Knowing only the core, the pattern can be extended. Knowing the number of steps in the core allows the identification of an item in each step without drawing/writing the entire pattern out. For example, suppose you must find the tenth item in the previous pattern. Because the core consists of three items (○○▲), the core repeats in multiples of 3. In other words, steps 3, 6, 9, 12, etc. will be ▲ completing the core with the core starting over on the next step. For the above example, the 9th step will be ▲ and the 10th will be ○.

The most common patterns where each item changes from one step to the next are arithmetic and geometric sequences. In an arithmetic sequence, the items increase or decrease by a constant difference. In other words, the same thing is added or subtracted to each item or step to produce the next. To determine if a sequence is arithmetic, see what must be added or subtracted to step one to produce step two. Then, check if the same thing is added/subtracted to step two to produce step three. The same thing must be added/subtracted to step three to produce step four, and so on. Consider the pattern 13, 10, 7, 4, ... To get from step one (13) to step two (10) requires subtracting by 3. The next step is checking if subtracting 3 from step two (10) will produce step three (7), and subtracting 3 from step three (7) will produce step four (4). In this case, the pattern holds true. Therefore, this is an arithmetic sequence in which each step is produced by subtracting 3 from the previous step. To extend the sequence, 3 is subtracted from the last step to produce the next. The next three numbers in the sequence are 1, -2, -5.

A geometric sequence is one in which each step is produced by multiplying or dividing the previous step by the same number. To see if a sequence is geometric, decide what step one must be multiplied or divided by to produce step two. Then check if multiplying or dividing step two by the same number produces step three, and so on. Consider the pattern 2, 8, 32, 128, ... To get from step one (2) to step two (8) requires multiplication by 4. The next step determines if multiplying step two (8) by 4 produces step three (32), and multiplying step three (32) by 4 produces step four (128). In this case, the pattern holds true. Therefore, this is a geometric sequence in which each step is found by multiplying the previous step by 4. To extend the sequence, the last step is multiplied by 4 and repeated. The next three numbers in the sequence are 512; 2,048; 8,192.

Arithmetic and geometric sequences can also be represented by shapes. For example, an arithmetic sequence could consist of shapes with three sides, four sides, and five sides. A geometric sequence could consist of eight blocks, four blocks, and two blocks (each step is produced by dividing the number of blocks in the previous step by 2).

Relationships Between the Corresponding Terms of Two Numerical Patterns

When given two number patterns, the corresponding terms should be examined to determine if a relationship exists between them. Corresponding terms between patterns are the pairs of numbers which appear in the same step of the two sequences. Consider the following patterns 1, 2, 3, 4,... and 3, 6, 9, 12, ... The corresponding terms are: 1 and 3; 2 and 6; 3 and 9; and 4 and 12. To identify the

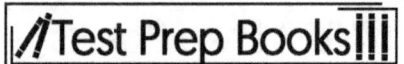

relationship, each pair of corresponding terms is examined. You can also examine the possibilities of performing an operation (+, −, ×, ÷) to each sequence. In this case:

$1 + 2 = 3$ or $1 \times 3 = 3$

$2 + 4 = 6$ or $2 \times 3 = 6$

$3 + 6 = 9$ or $3 \times 3 = 9$

$4 + 8 = 12$ or $4 \times 3 = 12$

The pattern is that the number from the first sequence multiplied by 3 equals the number in the second sequence. By assigning each sequence a label (input and output) or variable (x and y), the relationship can be written as an equation. The first sequence represents the inputs, or x, and the second sequence represents the outputs, or y. So, the relationship can be expressed as: $y = 3x$.

Consider the following sets of numbers:

a	2	4	6	8
b	6	8	10	12

To write a rule for the relationship between the values for *a* and the values for *b*, the corresponding terms (2 and 6; 4 and 8; 6 and 10; 8 and 12) are examined. The possibilities for producing *b* from *a* are:

$2 + 4 = 6$ or $2 \times 3 = 6$

$4 + 4 = 8$ or $4 \times 2 = 8$

$6 + 4 = 10$

$8 + 4 = 12$ or $8 \times 1.5 = 12$

The pattern is that adding 4 to the value of *a* produces the value of *b*. The relationship can be written as the equation $a + 4 = b$.

Basic Concepts of Geometry

Geometry is the part of mathematics that deals with shapes and their properties. It is also similar to measurement and number operations. The basis of geometry involves being able to label and describe shapes and their properties. That knowledge will lead to working with formulas such as area, perimeter, and volume. This knowledge will help to solve word problems involving shapes.

Flat or two-dimensional shapes include circles, triangles, hexagons, and rectangles, among others. Three-dimensional solid shapes, such as spheres and cubes, are also used in geometry. A shape can be classified based on whether it is open like the letter U or closed like the letter O. Further classifications involve counting the number of sides and vertices (corners) on the shapes. This will help you tell the difference between shapes.

Quantitative Section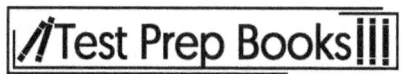

Polygons can be drawn by sketching a fixed number of line segments that meet to create a closed shape. In addition, *triangles* can be drawn by sketching a closed space using only three line segments. *Quadrilaterals* are closed shapes with four line segments. Note that a triangle has three vertices, and a quadrilateral has four vertices.

To draw circles, one curved line segment must be drawn that has only one endpoint. This creates a closed shape. Given such direction, every point on the line would be the same distance away from its center. The radius of a circle goes from an endpoint on the center of the circle to an endpoint on the circle. The diameter is the line segment created by placing an endpoint on the circle, drawing through the radius, and placing the other endpoint on the circle. A compass can be used to draw circles of a more precise size and shape.

Area and Perimeter

Area relates to two-dimensional geometric shapes. Basically, a figure is divided into two-dimensional units. The number of units needed to cover the figure is counted. Area is measured using square units, such as square inches, feet, centimeters, or kilometers.

Perimeter is the length of all its sides. The perimeter of a given closed sided figure would be found by first measuring the length of each side and then calculating the sum of all sides.

Formulas can be used to calculate area and perimeter. The area of a rectangle is found by multiplying its length, l, times its width, w. Therefore, the formula for area is $A = l \times w$. An equivalent expression is found by using the term base, b, instead of length, to represent the horizontal side of the shape. In this case, the formula is $A = b \times h$. This same formula can be used for all parallelograms. Here is a visualization of a rectangle with its labeled sides:

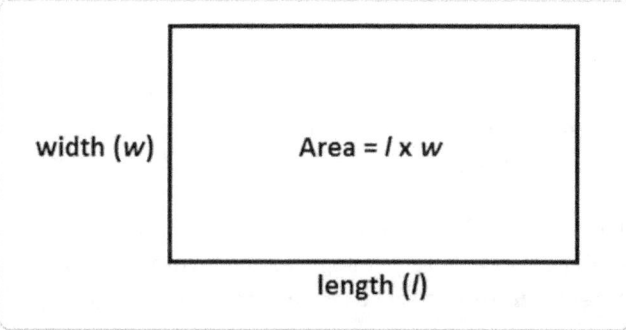

A square has four equal sides with the length s. Its length is equal to its width. The formula for the area of a square is $A = s \times s$. Finally, the area of a triangle is calculated by dividing the area of the rectangle that would be formed by the base, the altitude, and height of the triangle. Therefore, the area of a triangle is $A = \frac{1}{2} \times b \times h$. Formulas for perimeter are derived by adding length measurements of the sides of a figure. The perimeter of a rectangle is the result of adding the length of the four sides. Therefore, the formula for perimeter of a rectangle is $P = 2 \times l + 2 \times w$, and the formula for perimeter of a square is $P = 4 \times s$. The perimeter of a triangle would be the sum of the lengths of the three sides.

Volume

Volume is a measurement of the amount of space that in a 3-dimensional figure. Volume is measured using cubic units, such as cubic inches, feet, centimeters, or kilometers.

Say you have 10 playing die that are each one cubic centimeter. Say you placed these along the length of a rectangle. Then 8 die are placed along its width. The remaining area is filled in with die. There would be 80 die in total. This would equal a volume of 80 cubic centimeters. Say the shape is doubled so that its height consists of two cube lengths. There would be 160 cubes. Also, its volume would be 160 cubic centimeters. Adding another level of cubes would mean that there would be $3 \times 80 = 240$ cubes. This idea shows that volume is calculated by multiplying area times height. The actual formula for volume of a three-dimensional rectangular solid is $V = l \times w \times h$. In this formula *l* represents length, *w* represents width, and *h* represents height. Volume can also be thought of as area of the base times the height. The base in this case would be the entire rectangle formed by *l* and *w*. Here is an example of a rectangular solid with labeled sides:

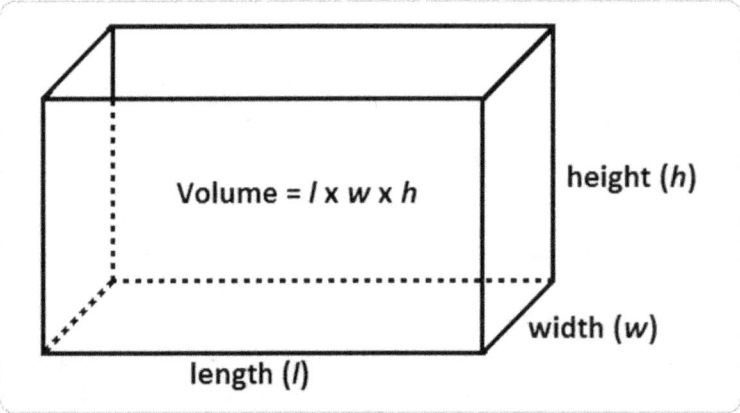

A *cube* is a special type of rectangular solid in which its length, width, and height are the same. If this length is *s*, then the formula for the volume of a cube is $V = s \times s \times s$.

Lines and Angles

In geometry, a *line* connects two points, has no thickness, and extends indefinitely in both directions beyond the points. If it does end at two points, it is known as a *line segment*. It is important to distinguish between a line and a line segment.

An angle can be visualized as a corner. It is defined as the formation of two rays connecting at a vertex that extend indefinitely. Angles are measured in degrees. Their measurement is a measure of rotation. A full rotation equals 360 degrees and represents a circle. Half of a rotation equals 180 degrees and represents a half-circle. Subsequently, 90 degrees represents a quarter-circle. Similar to the hands on a clock, an angle begins at the center point, and two lines extend indefinitely from that point in two different directions.

A clock can be useful when learning how to measure angles. At 3:00, the big hand is on the 12 and the small hand is on the 3. The angle formed is 90 degrees and is known as a *right angle*. Any angle less than 90 degrees, such as the one formed at 2:00, is known as an *acute angle*. Any angle greater than 90 degrees is known as an *obtuse angle*. The entire clock represents 360 degrees, and each clockwise increment on the clock represents an addition of 30 degrees. Therefore, 6:00 represents 180 degrees, 7:00 represents 210 degrees, etc. Angle measurement is additive. An angle can be broken into two non-overlapping angles. The total measure of the larger angle is equal to the sum of the measurements of the two smaller angles.

A *ray* is a straight path that has an endpoint on one end and extends indefinitely in the other direction. Lines are known as being *coplanar* if they are located in the same plane. Coplanar lines exist within the same two-dimensional surface. Two lines are *parallel* if they are coplanar, extend in the same direction, and never cross. They are known as being *equidistant* because they are always the same distance from each other. If lines do cross, they are known as *intersecting lines*. As discussed previously, angles are utilized throughout geometry, and their measurement can be seen through the use of an analog clock. An angle is formed when two rays begin at the same endpoint. *Adjacent angles* can be formed by forming two angles out of one shared ray. They are two side-by-side angles that also share an endpoint.

Perpendicular lines are coplanar lines that form a right angle at their point of intersection. A triangle that contains a right angle is known as a *right triangle*. The sum of the angles within any triangle is always 180 degrees. Therefore, in a right triangle, the sum of the two angles that are not right angles is 90 degrees. Any two angles that sum up to 90 degrees are known as *complementary angles*. A triangle that contains an obtuse angle is known as an *obtuse triangle*. A triangle that contains three acute angles is known as an *acute triangle*. Here is an example of a 180-degree angle, split up into an acute and obtuse angle:

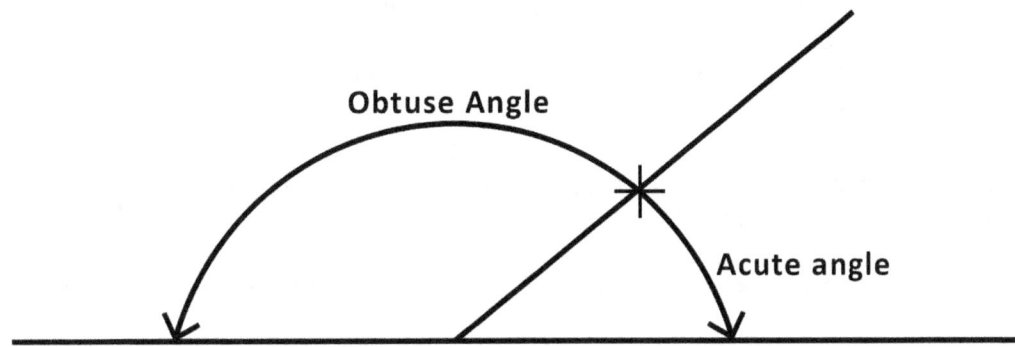

The vocabulary regarding many two-dimensional shapes is important to understand and use appropriately. Many four-sided figures can be identified using properties of angles and lines. A *quadrilateral* is a closed shape with four sides. A *parallelogram* is a specific type of quadrilateral that has two sets of parallel lines having the same length. A *trapezoid* is a quadrilateral having only one set of parallel sides. A *rectangle* is a parallelogram that has four right angles. A *rhombus* is a parallelogram with four equal sides and sometimes two acute angles and two obtuse angles. The acute angles are of equal measure, and the obtuse angles are of equal measure. Finally, a *square* is a rhombus consisting of four right angles. It is important to note that some of these shapes share common attributes. For instance, all four-sided shapes are quadrilaterals. All squares are rectangles, but not all rectangles are squares.

Symmetry is another concept in geometry. If a two-dimensional shape can be folded along a straight line and the halves line up exactly, the figure is *symmetric*. The line is known as a *line of symmetry*. Circles, squares, and rectangles are examples of symmetric shapes.

Basic Concepts of Measurement

Measurement is how an object's length, width, height, weight, and so on, are quantified. Measurement is related to counting, but it is a more refined process.

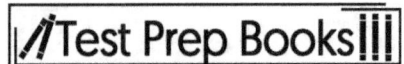

Quantitative Section

The standard units of length in the United States are *inches*, *feet*, and *yards*. Weight units can vary, based on whether the substance being measured is a liquid or a solid. Standard units of weight to measure liquids include *ounces*, *pints*, *quarts*, and *gallons*. Occasionally, solids can also be measured using pints and quarts. For example, both milk and berries can be measured in pints. Other units of weight are *pounds* and *tons*.

The *metric* system is another measurement system. It is used in most countries outside of the United States. Units of mass within the metric system are *milligrams*, *grams*, and *kilograms*. Units of volume within the metric system are *milliliters* and *liters*. Finally, units of length within the metric system are *centimeters*, *meters*, and *kilometers*. Some other measures that are important are when you bake, such as *teaspoons*, *tablespoons*, and *cups*, or measuring temperature in *Celsius* and *Fahrenheit*. When discussing measurements, including proper units is crucial.

Telling time is another important measurement and real-world application. You should memorize units of time such as *seconds, minutes, hours, days*, and *years*. For example, there are 60 seconds in a minute, 60 minutes in each hour, and 24 hours in a day.

Converting units within either the United States units of measure or the metric system is important in real-world application problems. You should always make sure that values are converted to the same units before you begin the operation. If two lengths are added that have different units, the answer would not make sense. Some length conversions within the U.S. system are that one foot is 12 inches, one yard is 3 feet, and one mile is 5,280 feet. Some length conversions within the metric system are that one centimeter is 10 millimeters, one meter is 100 centimeters, and one kilometer is 1,000 meters. In terms of volume, one liter is 1,000 milliliters.

Tools, such as rulers, yardsticks, and measuring tapes, can be used to measure and compare the length of objects.

In order to determine the length of an object, it should be measured from end of the object to the other. Distance measurement is the same idea. Distance equals a measurement from the beginning to the end, with no gaps in between. Subtraction needs to be used to determine how much shorter an object is when compared to another object.

When you come across a measurement problem, pay attention to what units the final answer needs to be written in. All measurements should be converted to the same units before any calculations are completed. For example, if measurements are provided in both inches and feet, and the end result must be in inches, the measurements in feet must be converted to inches.

Interpretation of Graphs

Data can be represented in many ways including picture graphs, bar graphs, line plots, and tally charts. It is important to be able to organize the data into categories that could be represented using one of these methods. Equally important is the ability to read these types of diagrams and interpret their meaning.

A *picture graph* is a diagram that shows pictorial representations of data being discussed. The symbols used can represent a certain number of objects.

Notice how each fruit symbol in the following graph represents a count of two fruits. One drawback of picture graphs is that they can be less accurate if each symbol represents a large number. For example,

Quantitative Section

if each banana symbol represented ten bananas, and students consumed 22 bananas, it may be challenging to draw and interpret two and one-fifth bananas as a frequency count of 22.

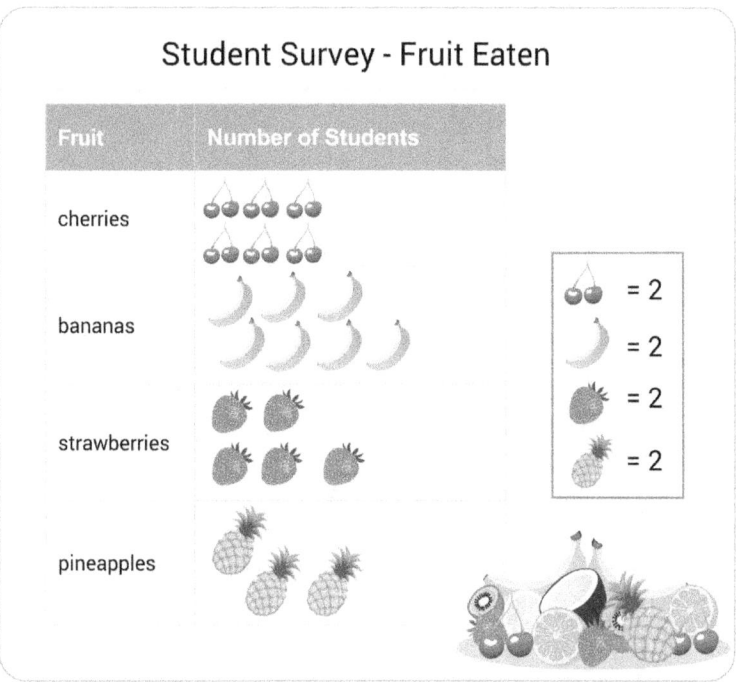

A *bar graph* is a diagram in which the quantity of items within a specific classification is represented by the height of a rectangle. Each type of classification is represented by a rectangle of equal width. Here is an example of a bar graph:

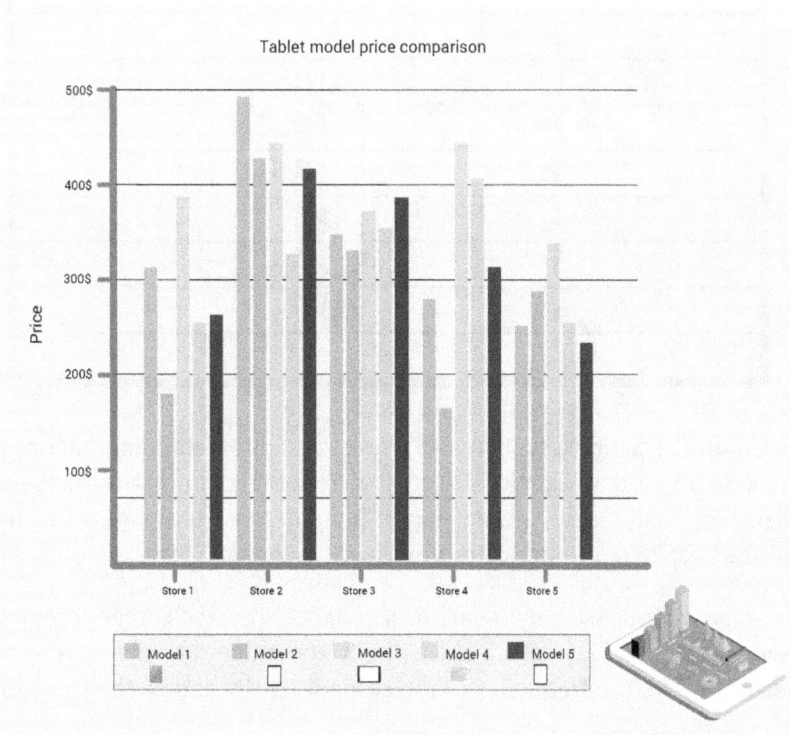

A *line plot* is a diagram that shows quantity of data along a number line. It is a quick way to record data in a structure similar to a bar graph without needing to do the required shading of a bar graph. Here is an example of a line plot:

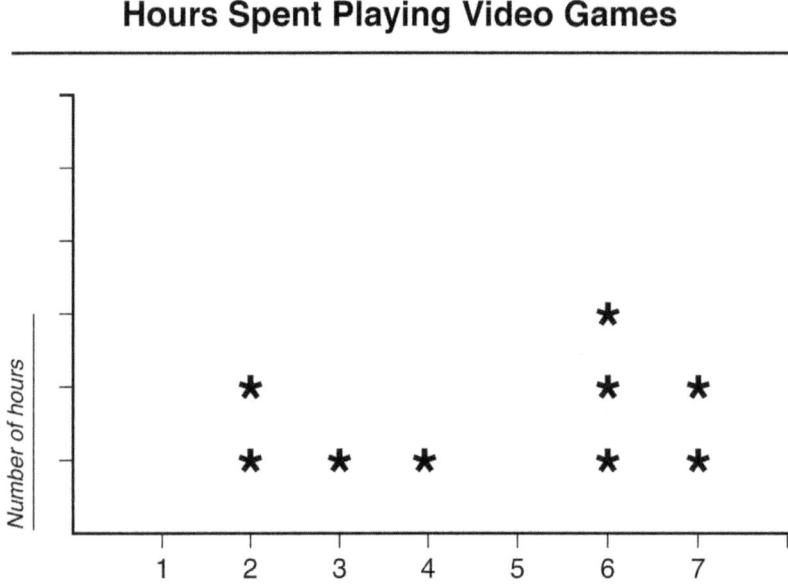

A *tally chart* is a diagram in which tally marks are utilized to represent data. Tally marks are a means of showing a quantity of objects within a specific classification. Here is an example of a tally chart:

Number of days with rain	Number of weeks
0	||
1	⑷ |
2	⑷ ||||
3	⑷ ⑷ ⑷
4	⑷
5	⑷ |
6	⑷
7	|

Data is often recorded using fractions, such as half a mile, and understanding fractions is critical because of their popular use in real-world applications. Also, it is extremely important to label values with their units when using data. For example, regarding length, the number 2 is meaningless unless it is attached to a unit. A measurement of 2 cm is much different than 2 miles.

A circle graph, also called a pie chart, shows categorical data with each category representing a percentage of the whole data set. To make a circle graph, the percent of the data set for each category must be determined. To do so, the frequency of the category is divided by the total number of data

Quantitative Section

points and converted to a percent. For example, if 80 people were asked what their favorite sport is and 20 responded basketball, basketball makes up 25% of the data ($\frac{20}{80} = 0.25 = 25\%$). Each category in a data set is represented by a *slice* of the circle proportionate to its percentage of the whole.

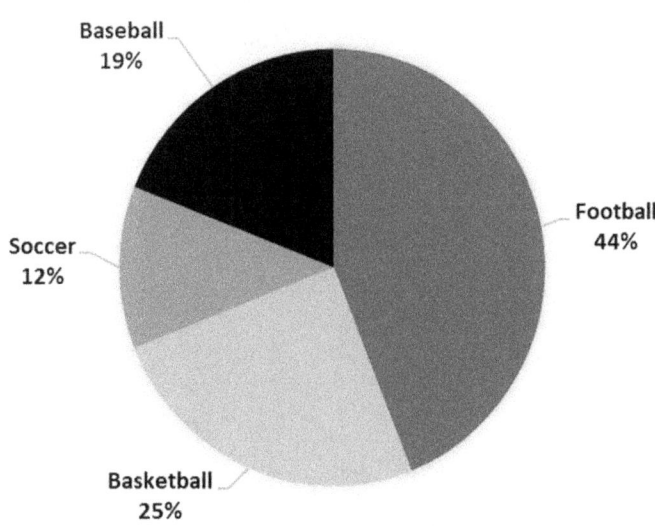

A scatter plot displays the relationship between two variables. Values for the independent variable, typically denoted by *x*, are paired with values for the dependent variable, typically denoted by *y*. Each set of corresponding values are written as an ordered pair (*x*, *y*). To construct the graph, a coordinate grid is labeled with the *x*-axis representing the independent variable and the *y*-axis representing the dependent variable. Each ordered pair is graphed.

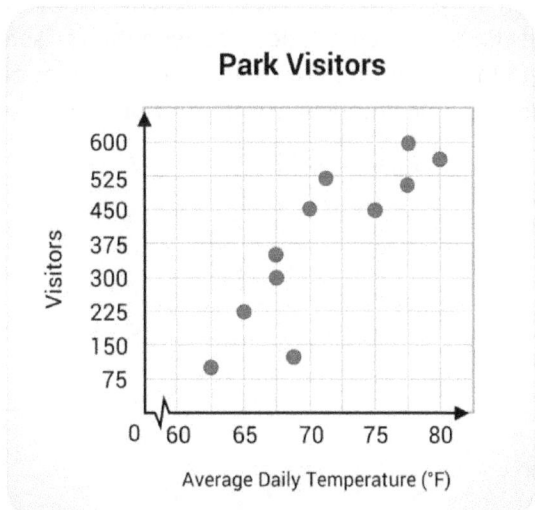

Like a scatter plot, a line graph compares two variables that change continuously, typically over time. Paired data values (ordered pairs) are plotted on a coordinate grid with the *x*- and *y*-axis representing the two variables. A line is drawn from each point to the next, going from left to right. A double line graph simply displays two sets of data that contain values for the same two variables. The double line graph below displays the profit for given years (two variables) for Company A and Company B (two data sets).

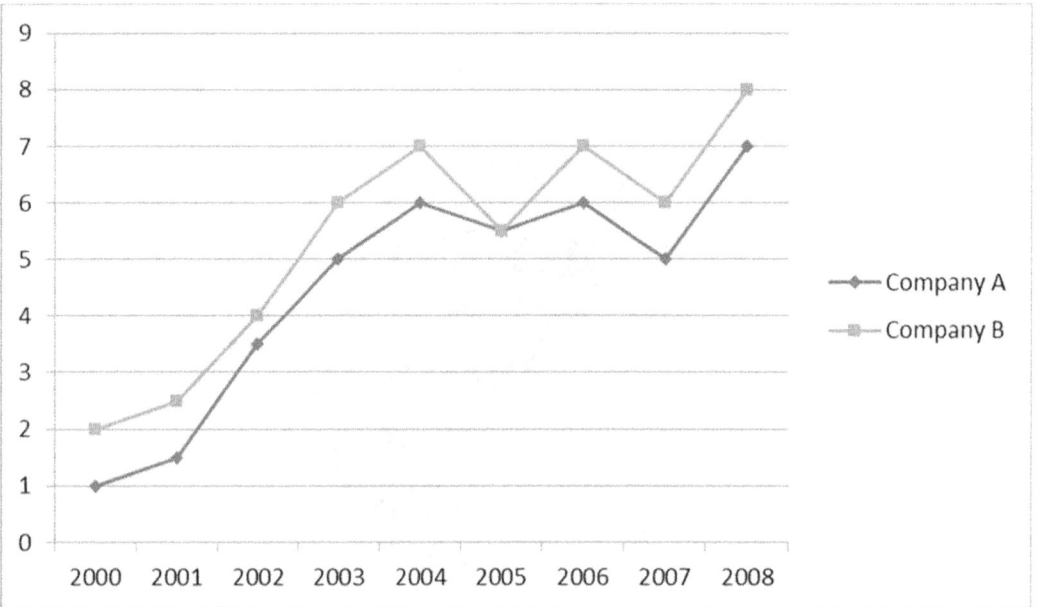

Choosing the appropriate graph to display a data set depends on what type of data is included in the set and what information must be shown. Histograms and box plots can be used for data sets consisting of individual values across a wide range. Examples include test scores and incomes. Histograms and box plots will indicate the center, spread, range, and outliers of a data set. A histogram will show the shape of the data set, while a box plot will divide the set into quartiles (25% increments), allowing for comparison between a given value and the entire set.

Scatter plots and line graphs can be used to display data consisting of two variables. Examples include height and weight, or distance and time. A correlation between the variables is determined by examining the points on the graph. Line graphs are used if each value for one variable pairs with a distinct value for the other variable. Line graphs show relationships between variables.

Practice Quiz

1. Which is closest to 17.8×9.9?
    a. 140
    b. 180
    c. 200
    d. 300
    e. 400

2. Which of the following numbers has the greatest value?
    a. 1.43785
    b. 1.07548
    c. 1.43592
    d. 0.89409
    e. 0.909

3. The value of 6×12 is the same as:
    a. $2 \times 4 \times 4 \times 2$
    b. $7 \times 4 \times 3$
    c. $6 \times 6 \times 3$
    d. $3 \times 3 \times 4 \times 2$
    e. $6 \times 1 \times 2$

4. This chart indicates how many sales of CDs, vinyl records, and MP3 downloads occurred over the last year. Approximately what percentage of the total sales was from CDs?

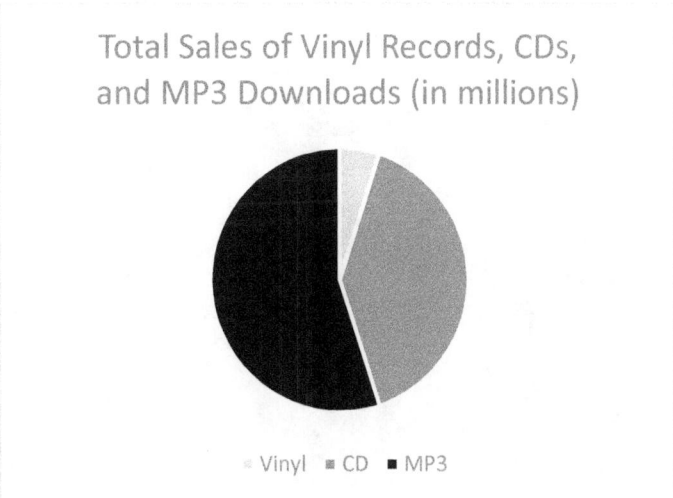

    a. 55%
    b. 25%
    c. 40%
    d. 5%
    e. 80%

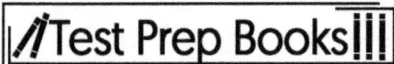

5. Which of the following values is the largest?
    a. 0.45
    b. 0.096
    c. 0.3
    d. 0.313
    e. 0.009

See answers on the next page.

Answer Explanations

1. B: Instead of multiplying these out, we can estimate the product by using $18 \times 10 = 180$.

2. A: Compare each number after the decimal point to figure out which overall number is greatest. In Choices A (1.43785) and C (1.43592), both have the same tenths place (4) and hundredths place (3). However, the thousandths place is greater in Choice A (7), so it has the greatest value overall.

3. D: By rearranging and grouping the factors in Choice D, we can notice that $3 \times 3 \times 4 \times 2 = (3 \times 2) \times (4 \times 3) = 6 \times 12$, which is what we were looking for.

4. C: The total percentage of a pie chart equals 100%. We can see that CD sales make up less than half of the chart (50%) but more than a quarter (25%), and the only answer choice that meets these criteria is Choice C, 40%.

5. A: To figure out which value is the largest, look at the first nonzero digits. Choice B's first nonzero digit is in the hundredths place. The other three all have nonzero digits in the tenths place, so it must be Choice A, C, or D. Of these, Choice A's first nonzero digit is the largest.

Verbal Section

Test takers encounter two parts in the verbal section of the Elementary SSAT. In the first part, the vocabulary section, questions address the test taker's understanding of language and the meanings of different words. The second part is the analogy section, which assesses the test taker's understanding of the finer details in the relationships of different words.

Vocabulary

Vocabulary is the words a person uses on a daily basis. Having a good vocabulary is important. It's important in writing and also when you talk to people. Many of the questions on the test may have words that you don't know. Therefore, it's important to learn ways to find out a word's meaning.

It's hard to use vocabulary correctly. Imagine being thrust into a foreign country. If you didn't know right words to use to ask for the things you need, you could run into trouble! Asking for help from people who don't share the same vocabulary is hard. Language helps us understand each other. The more vocabulary words a person knows, the easier they can ask for things they need. This section of the study guide focuses on getting to know vocabulary through basic grammar.

Prefixes and Suffixes

In this section, we will look at the *meaning* of various prefixes and suffixes when added to a root word. A *prefix* is a combination of letters found at the beginning of a word. A *suffix* is a combination of letters found at the end. A *root word* is the word that comes after the prefix, before the suffix, or between them both. Sometimes a root word can stand on its own without either a prefix or a suffix. More simply put:

Prefix + Root Word = Word

Root Word + Suffix = Word

Prefix + Root Word + Suffix = Word

Root Word = Word

Knowing the definitions of common prefixes and suffixes is helpful. It's helpful when you are trying to find out the meaning of a word you don't know. Also, knowing prefixes can help you find out the number of things, the negative of something, or the time and space of an object! Understanding suffixes can help when trying to find out the meaning of an adjective, noun, or verb.

The following charts look at some of the most common prefixes, what they mean, and how they're used to find out a word's meaning:

Number and Quantity Prefixes

Prefix	Definition	Example
bi-	two	bicycle, bilateral
mono-	one, single	monopoly, monotone
poly-	many	polygamy, polygon
semi-	half, partly	semiannual, semicircle
uni-	one	unicycle, universal

Here's an example of a number prefix:

The girl rode on a *bicycle* to school.

Look at the word *bicycle*. The root word (*cycle*) comes from the Greek and means *wheel*. The prefix *bi-* means *two*. The word *bicycle* means two wheels! When you look at any bicycles, they all have two wheels. If you had a unicycle, your bike would only have one wheel, because *uni-* means *one*.

Negative Prefixes

Prefix	Definition	Example
a-	without, lack of	amoral, atypical
in-	not, opposing	inability, inverted
non-	not	nonexistent, nonstop
un-	not, reverse	unable, unspoken

Here's an example of a negative prefix:

The girl was *insensitive* to the boy who broke his leg.

Look at the word *insensitive*. In the chart above, the prefix *in-* means *not* or *opposing*. Replace the prefix with *not*. Now place *not* in front of the word *sensitive*. Now we see that the girl was "not sensitive" to the boy who broke his leg. In simpler terms, she showed that she did not care. These are easy ways to use prefixes and suffixes in order to find out what a word means.

Time and Space Prefixes

Prefix	Definition	Example
a-	in, on, of, up, to	aloof, associate
ab-	from, away, off	abstract, absent
ad-	to, towards	adept, adjacent
ante-	before, previous	antebellum, antenna
anti-	against, opposing	anticipate, antisocial
cata-	down, away, thoroughly	catacomb, catalogue
circum-	around	circumstance, circumvent
com-	with, together, very	combine, compel
contra-	against, opposing	contraband, contrast
de-	from	decrease, descend
dia-	through, across, apart	diagram, dialect
dis-	away, off, down, not	disregard, disrespect
epi-	upon	epidemic, epiphany
ex-	out	example, exit
hypo-	under, beneath	hypoallergenic, hypothermia
inter-	among, between	intermediate, international
intra-	within	intrapersonal, intravenous
ob-	against, opposing	obtain, obscure
per-	through	permanent, persist
peri-	around	periodontal, periphery
post-	after, following	postdate, postoperative

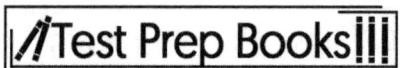

Verbal Section

Prefix	Definition	Example
pre-	before, previous	precede, premeditate
pro-	forward, in place of	program, propel
retro-	back, backward	retroactive, retrofit
sub-	under, beneath	submarine, substantial
super-	above, extra	superior, supersede
trans-	Across, beyond, or over	transform, transmit
ultra-	beyond, excessively	ultraclean, ultralight

Here's an example of a space prefix:

> The teacher's motivational speech helped *propel* her students toward greater academic achievement.

Look at the word *propel*. The prefix *pro-* means *forward*. *Forward* means something related to time and space. *Propel* means to drive or move in a forward direction. Therefore, knowing the prefix *pro-* helps interpret that the students are moving forward *toward greater academic achievement*.

Miscellaneous Prefixes

Prefix	Definition	Example
belli-	war, warlike	bellied, belligerent
bene-	well, good	benediction, beneficial
equi-	equal	equidistant, equinox
for-	away, off, from	forbidden, forsaken
fore-	previous	forecast, forebode
homo-	same, equal	homogeneous, homonym
hyper-	excessive, over	hyperextend, hyperactive
in-	in, into	insignificant, invasive
magn-	large	magnetic, magnificent
mal-	bad, poorly, not	maladapted, malnourished
mis-	bad, poorly, not	misplace, misguide
mor-	death	mortal, morgue
neo-	new	neoclassical, neonatal
omni-	all, everywhere	omnipotent, omnipresent
ortho-	right, straight	orthodontist, orthopedic
over-	above	overload, overstock,
pan-	all, entire	panacea, pander
para-	beside, beyond	paradigm, parameter
phil-	love, like	philanthropy, philosophic
prim-	first, early	primal, primer
re-	backward, again	reload, regress
sym-	with, together	symmetry, symbolize
vis-	to see	visual, visibility

Here's another prefix example:

> The computer was *primitive*; it still had a floppy disk drive!

Verbal Section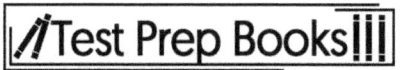

The word *primitive* has the prefix *prim-*. The prefix *prim-* indicates being *first* or *early*. *Primitive* means the early stages of evolution. It also could mean the historical development of something. Therefore, the sentence is saying that the computer is an older model, because it no longer has a floppy disk drive.

The charts that follow review some of the most common suffixes. They also include examples of how the suffixes that are used to determine the meaning of a word. Remember, suffixes are added to the *end* of a root word:

Adjective Suffixes

Suffix	Definition	Example
-able (-ible)	capable of being	teachable, accessible
-esque	in the style of, like	humoresque, statuesque
-ful	filled with, marked by	helpful, deceitful
-ic	having, containing	manic, elastic
-ish	suggesting, like	malnourish, tarnish
-less	lacking, without	worthless, fearless
-ous	marked by, given to	generous, previous

Here's an example of an adjective suffix:

The live model looked so *statuesque* in the window display; she didn't even move!

Look at the word *statuesque*. The suffix *-esque* means *in the style of* or *like*. If something is *statuesque*, it's *like a statue*. In this sentence, the model looks like a statue.

Noun Suffixes

Suffix	Definition	Example
-acy	state, condition	literacy, legacy
-ance	act, condition, fact	distance, importance
-ard	one that does	leotard, billiard
-ation	action, state, result	legislation, condemnation
-dom	state, rank, condition	freedom, kingdom
-er (-or)	office, action	commuter, spectator
-ess	feminine	caress, princess
-hood	state, condition	childhood, livelihood
-ion	action, result, state	communion, position
-ism	act, manner, doctrine	capitalism, patriotism
-ist	worker, follower	stylist, activist
-ity (-ty)	state, quality, condition	community, dirty
-ment	result, action	empowerment, segment
-ness	quality, state	fitness, rudeness
-ship	position	censorship, leadership
-sion (-tion)	state, result	tension, transition
-th	act, state, quality	twentieth, wealth
-tude	quality, state, result	attitude, latitude

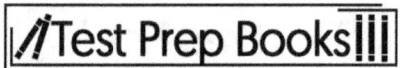

Look at the following example of a noun suffix:

The *spectator* cheered when his favorite soccer team scored a goal.

Look at the word *spectator*. The suffix *-or* means *action*. In this sentence, the *action* is to *spectate* (watch something). Therefore, a *spectator* is someone involved in watching something.

Verb Suffixes

Suffix	Definition	Example
-ate	having, showing	facilitate, integrate
-en	cause to be, become	frozen, written
-fy	make, cause to have	modify, rectify
-ize	cause to be, treat with	realize, sanitize

Here's an example of a verb suffix:

The preschool had to *sanitize* the toys every Tuesday and Thursday.

In the word *sanitize*, the suffix *-ize* means *cause to be* or *treat with*. By adding the suffix *-ize* to the root word *sanitary*, the meaning of the word becomes active: *cause to be sanitary*.

Context Clues

It's common to find words that aren't familiar in writing. When you don't know a word, there are some "tricks" that can be used to find out its meaning. *Context clues* are words or phrases in a sentence or paragraph that provide hints about a word and what it means. For example, if an unknown word is attached to a noun with other surrounding words as clues, these can help you figure out the word's meaning. Consider the following example:

After the treatment, Grandma's natural rosy cheeks looked *wan* and ghostlike.

The word we don't know is *wan*. The first clue to its meaning is in the phrase *After the treatment*, which tells us that something happened after a procedure (possibly medical). A second clue is the word *rosy*, which describes Grandma's natural cheek color that changed after the treatment. Finally, the word *ghostlike* infers that Grandma's cheeks now look white. By using the context clues in the sentence, we can figure out that the meaning of the word *wan* means *pale*.

Below are more ways to use context clues to find out the meaning of a word we don't know:

Contrasts

Look for context clues that *contrast* the unknown word. When reading a sentence with a word we don't know, look for an opposite word or idea. Here's an example:

Since Mary didn't cite her research sources, she lost significant points for *plagiarizing* the content of her report.

In this sentence, *plagiarizing* is the word we don't know. Notice that when Mary *didn't cite her research sources,* it resulted in her losing points for *plagiarizing the content of her report*. These contrasting ideas tell us that Mary did something wrong with the content. This makes sense because the definition of *plagiarizing* is "taking the work of someone else and passing it off as your own."

Verbal Section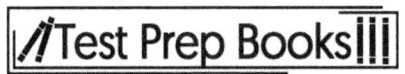

Contrasts often use words like *but, however, although,* or phrases like *on the other hand.* For example:

The *gargantuan* television won't fit in my car, but it will cover the entire wall in the den.

The word we don't know is *gargantuan*. Notice that the television is too big to fit in a car, <u>*but* it will cover the entire wall in the den</u>. This tells us that the television is extremely large. The word *gargantuan* means *enormous*.

Synonyms

Another way to find out a word you don't know is to think of synonyms for that word. Synonyms are words with the same meaning. To do this, replace synonyms one at a time. Then read the sentence after each synonym to see if the meaning is clear. By replacing a word we don't know with a word we do know, it's easier to uncover its meaning. For example:

Gary's clothes were *saturated* after he fell into the swimming pool.

In this sentence, we don't know the word *saturated*. To brainstorm synonyms for *saturated*, think about what happens to Gary's clothes after falling into the swimming pool. They'd be *soaked* or *wet*. These both turn out to be good synonyms to try. The actual meaning of *saturated* is "thoroughly soaked."

Antonyms

Sometimes sentences contain words or phrases that oppose each other. Opposite words are known as *antonyms*. An example of an antonym is *hot* and *cold*. For example:

Although Mark seemed *tranquil*, you could tell he was actually nervous as he paced up and down the hall.

The word we don't know is *tranquil*. The sentence says that Mark was in fact not *tranquil*. He was *actually nervous*. The opposite of the word *nervous* is *calm*. *Calm* is the meaning of the word *tranquil*.

Explanations or Descriptions

Explanations or descriptions of other things in the sentence can also provide clues to an unfamiliar word. Take the following example:

Golden Retrievers, Great Danes, and Pugs are the top three *breeds* competing in the dog show.

We don't know the word *breeds*. Look at the sentence for a clue. The subjects (*Golden Retrievers, Great Danes*, and *Pugs*) describe different types of dogs. This description helps uncover the meaning of the word *breeds*. The word *breeds* means "a particular type of animal."

Inferences

Inferences are clues to an unknown word that tell us its meaning. These inferences can be found within the sentence where the word appears. Or, they can be found in a sentence before the word or after the word. Look at the following example:

The *wretched* old lady was kicked out of the restaurant. She was so mean and nasty to the waiter!

Here, we don't know the word *wretched*. The first sentence says that the *old lady was kicked out of the restaurant*, but it doesn't say why. The sentence after tells us why: *She was so mean and nasty to the*

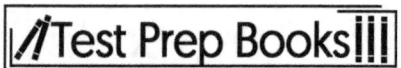

waiter! This infers that the old lady was *kicked out* because she was *so mean and nasty* or, in other words, *wretched*.

When you prepare for a vocabulary test, try reading harder materials to learn new words. If you don't know a word on the test, look for prefixes and suffixes to find out what the word means and get rid of wrong answers. If two answers both seem right, see if there are any differences between them. Then select the word that best fits. Context clues in the sentence or paragraph can also help you find the meaning of a word you don't know. By learning new words, a person can expand their knowledge. They can also improve the quality of their writing.

Analogies

Analogies compare two different things that are related to each other. For example, a basic analogy is: apple is to fruit as cucumber is to vegetable. This analogy points out the category each item belongs to. On the SSAT, the final term (vegetable, in this case) will be blank. The blank must be filled in from the choices. You must select the word that best shows the relationship in the first pair of words.

Other analogies include words that are synonyms. Synonyms are words that mean the same thing. For example, *big* and *large* are synonyms. *Tired* and *sleepy* are also synonyms. Verbal analogy questions can be hard. After practice, you will see small differences between word meanings and how they connect to each other.

Not all analogies are synonyms. Some analogies are *antonyms,* or words that are opposites. One example of an antonym is: fast as to slow as high is to low. Fast is the opposite of slow, and high is the opposite of low.

Analogies can also tell us the characteristics of things. An example of this is: pickle is to salty as candy is to sweet. Here the adjectives (salty and sweet) describe qualities of the foods.

Analogies also include people who use things and things that are used. For example: crayon is to draw as axe is the chop. This gives us a tool and then tells us what it is used for. The tools may also be linked tithe person who uses the device. For example, brush is to painter as hoe is to farmer. Painters use brushes to paint and farmers use hoes on the farm. Similarly, products are often linked to their producer. An example is: muffin is to baker as statue is to sculpture. The test taker must be familiar with the occupations to pick the right relationship.

Other analogies link parts of an object to the whole. An example is: fingers are to hand as toes are to foot. Or, bark is to tree as husk is to corn. With this last category mentioned, test takers must try to establish the precise relationship between the first two items when choosing the missing item in the second pair. For example, consider the following analogy and answer choices:

Bark is to tree as _____ is to hand.
   a. Fingers
   b. Skin
   c. Leaves
   d. Finger nails

Without thinking carefully, test takers may select Choice *A*: fingers. After all, trees *have* bark and hands *have* fingers. However, the relationship between bark and the tree should be more precisely defined as

Verbal Section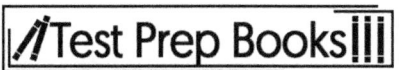

this: bark *covers* the tree. Then, careful test takers would select Choice *B*: skin. Skin covers the hand just like bark covers the tree.

The last types of analogy on the SSAT have to do with *homonyms* or rhyming words. Homonyms are words that are spelled differently but they sound the same. An example is four and for or bear and bare.

An analogy with rhyming words may *be sound is to pound as chair is to bear.* Sometimes it is helpful to read the analogies out loud quietly. The relationship may be in how the words sound, which can be harder to imagine.

It's also important to pay attention to the word order of each analogy question. Let's look at the following difficult question:

Carpenter is to saw as _____.
    a. Paint is to brush
    b. Painter is to mural
    c. Painter is to brush
    d. Brush is to painter

The correct answer is *C*: painter is to brush, because carpenters use saws for their tools and painters use brushes. Choice *D* reverses the order of the tool and the user, making the analogy false.

Practice Quiz

Synonyms

Each of the questions below has one word, followed by five other words. Please select one answer whose meaning is closest to the word in capital letters.

1. RESEARCH
    a. Criticize
    b. Change
    c. Teach
    d. Investigate
    e. Science

2. LUXURIOUS
    a. Faded
    b. Bright
    c. Fancy
    d. Inconsiderate
    e. Ordinary

Analogies

The questions below ask you to find relationships between words. For each question, select the answer that best completes the meaning of the sentence.

3. Dancing is to rhythm as singing is to
    a. Pitch.
    b. Mouth.
    c. Sound.
    d. Volume.
    e. Words.

4. Towel is to dry as hat is to
    a. Cold.
    b. Warm.
    c. Expose.
    d. Cover.
    e. Top.

5. Backpacks are to textbooks as
    a. Houses are to people.
    b. Fences are to trees.
    c. Plates are to food.
    d. Chalkboards are to chalk.
    e. Computers are to mice.

Answer Explanations

1. D: Research is closest in meaning to *investigate*. When someone does research, they look things up in different resources like books and journals, or they may conduct a scientific study, which is also called an investigation.

2. C: *Fancy* is the best synonym for *luxurious*—both describe elaborate and/or elegant lifestyles and/or settings.

3. A: This is a characteristic analogy. The connection lies in what observers will judge a performance on. While the other choices are also important, an off-key singer is as unpleasant as a dancer with no rhythm.

4. D: This is a use/tool analogy. The analogy focuses on an item's use. While hats are worn when it's cold with the goal of making the top of your head warm, this is not always guaranteed—their primary use is to provide cover. There is also the fact that not all hats are used to keep warm, but all hats cover the head.

5. A: This is a tool/use analogy. The key detail of this analogy is the idea of enclosing or sealing items/people. When plates are filled with food, there is no way to enclose the item. While trees can be inside a fence, they can also be specifically outside of one.

Reading Section

In the Reading section, you will have seven short passages. Each passage has four multiple-choice questions. The passages may be poetry, fiction, and nonfiction writing from many subjects. You may be asked to find word definitions or main ideas and supporting details. You may also be asked what literal language is opposed to non literal language.

Reading comprehension is being able to understand what you've read. Reading skills include fluency, vocabulary knowledge, and background knowledge. Fluency is the pace at which one reads. Background knowledge is the information you know about the passage before you've read it. These are all great building blocks that good readers use.

Good readers practice these skills before, during, and after reading. Before readers go through a passage, they should ask the following questions: "What do I already know about this subject?" and "What will the book be about?" While reading the passage, you should imagine the text. You should also use new information to make predictions. You can make connections to a personal experience. Or you can connect what you've read to another story. After reading a passage, you should be able to summarize the main idea. Good readers are able to retell the story in their own words.

Six Types of Comprehension Strategies

1. QUESTION	2. CONNECT	3. INFER
Monitor reading by asking questions before, during, and after reading a passage. "What if?," "I don't understand why," or "Maybe when" are all examples of how to use questions while reading.	Use knowledge to help with understanding text. Connecting with other stories or experiences is a way to help with reading comprehension. "This reminds me of … because" and "When I heard … it reminds me of" are both examples of how to connect with passages.	When authors do not give a clear answer, it sometimes helps to infer what happens in the passage. Inferring helps with making predictions, drawing conclusions, and reflecting on text. "I think," "Maybe," and "Perhaps" are all examples of ways to infer while reading.
4. VISUALIZE	**5. WHAT'S IMPORTANT**	**6. SYNTHESIZE**
Create pictures in the mind about the text. "I see," "It must have smelled like," and "I can imagine" are all examples of how to visualize while reading.	Determine the author's main idea. "The main idea is," "This section is mainly about," and "It is important to remember" are all examples of how to determine what is important while reading.	Combine current knowledge with new information to help with text understanding. "After reviewing," "At first I thought," and "Now I think" are all examples of how to synthesize information while reading.

Topic Versus the Main Idea

It is important to know the difference between the topic and the main idea of the passage. Even though these two are similar, they have some differences. A topic is the subject of the text. It can usually be described in a one- to two-word phrase. On the other hand, the main idea is more detailed. It provides the author's central point of the passage. It can be expressed through a complete sentence. It is often found in the beginning, middle, or end of a paragraph. In most nonfiction books, the first sentence of the passage usually states the main idea. Take a look at the passage below to review the topic versus the main idea.

> Cheetahs are one of the fastest mammals on land, reaching up to seventy miles an hour over short distances. Even though cheetahs can run as fast as seventy miles an hour, they usually only have to run half that speed to catch up with their choice of prey. Cheetahs cannot maintain a fast pace over long periods of time because they will overheat their bodies. After a chase, cheetahs need to rest for approximately thirty minutes prior to eating or returning to any other activity.

In the example above, the topic of the passage is Cheetahs because that is the subject of the text. The main idea of the text is "Cheetahs are one of the fastest mammals on the land but can only maintain a fast pace for shorter distances." While this covers the topic, it is more detailed. It refers to the text in its entirety. The passage provides more details called supporting details. These will be discussed in the next section.

Supporting Details

Supporting details help you understand the main idea. Supporting details answer questions like *who, what, where, when, why,* and *how.* Supporting details can include examples, facts, statistics, small stories, and visual details.

Persuasive and informative texts often use supporting details. In persuasive texts, authors try to make readers agree with their points of view. In persuasive texts, supporting details are often used as "selling points." If authors say something, they should support it with evidence. This helps to persuade readers. Informative texts use supporting details to inform readers. Take another look at the "Cheetahs" example from the page before to find examples of supporting details.

In the Cheetah example above, supporting details include:

- Cheetahs reach up to seventy miles per hour over short distances.
- Cheetahs usually only have to run half that speed to catch up with their prey.
- Cheetahs will overheat their bodies if they exert a high speed over longer distances.
- They need to rest for thirty minutes after a chase.

Look at the diagram below (applying the cheetah example) to help determine the hierarchy of topic, main idea, and supporting details.

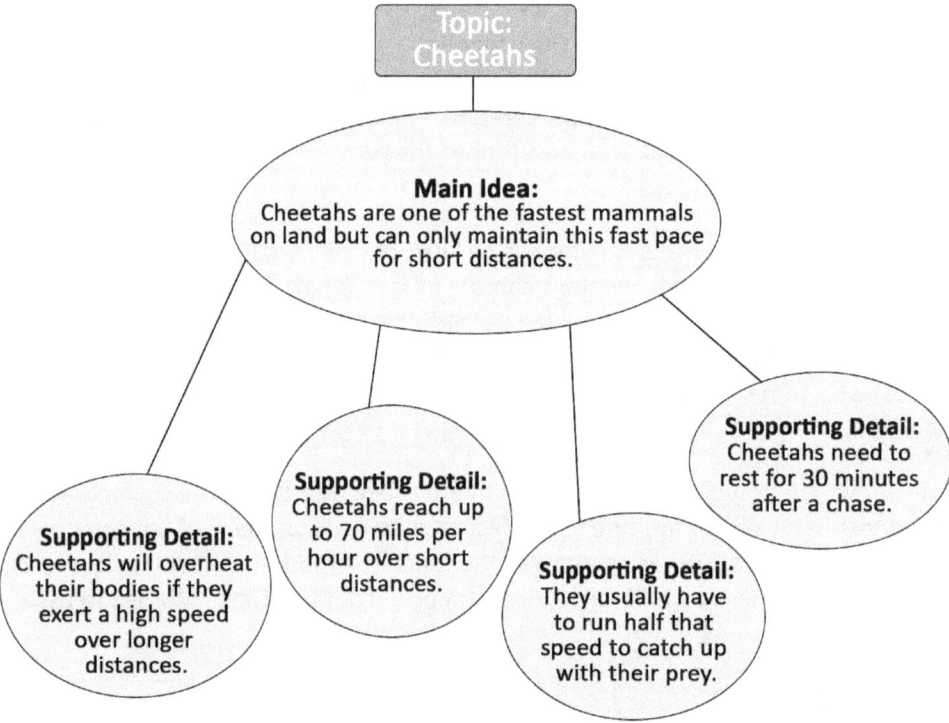

Theme

The theme is the central message of the story. The theme can be about a moral or lesson that the author wants to share with the readers. Although authors do not directly state the theme of a story, it is the "big picture" that they want readers to walk away with. For example, the fairy tale "The Boy Who Cried Wolf" is the tale of a little boy who always lied about seeing a wolf. When the little boy really saw a wolf, no one believed him. The author of this fairy tale does not tell readers, "Don't lie because people will question the truth of the story." However, the author presents this moral through the tale.

The themeof a text can center around varying subjects such as courage, friendship, love, bravery, facing challenges, or adversity. It often leaves readers with more questions than answers. Authors tend to imply certain themes in texts. However, readers are left to find out the true meaning of the story.

Purposes for Writing

Authors want readers to like their story. A good reader listens to what an author has to say. An author's purpose may be to persuade, inform, entertain, or be descriptive. Most stories are written to entertain the reader. Some stories may also be informative or persuasive. When an author wants to persuade the reader, the reader must be careful. The author may want to keep the persuasion lighthearted and friendly to maintain the entertainment. However, the author may still be trying to convince the reader of something, even if the story seems just for fun.

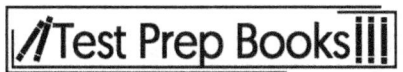

Informative texts means that the author is trying to educate the reader on a certain topic. Informative texts are usually nonfiction, which means they are true. The author doesn't state their opinion in an informative text. They simply tell you the facts to inform you. Some informative texts have headings, subtitles and bold key words. The purpose of informative texts is to educate the reader.

Entertaining texts can be fiction or nonfiction. They are meant to capture your attention. Entertaining texts are stories that describe real or fictional people, places or things. These stories use exciting language, emotion, and imagery. They also use figurative language. If an author writes a good entertaining text, you will never want to put the book down!

Descriptive texts describe people, places, or things to show a clear image to the reader. If an author fails to show these details, readers may find it boring or confusing. Descriptive texts are almost always informative. But they can also be persuasive or entertaining. It depends on the author's purpose.

Writing Devices

Authors use a variety of writing devices throughout texts. Below is a list of some writing devices authors use in their writing.

- Comparison and Contrast
- Cause and Effect
- Analogy
- Point of View
- Transitional Words and Phrases

Let's look at each device individually.

Comparison and Contrast

One writing device authors use is comparison and contrast. Comparison is when authors take objects and show how they are the same. Contrast is when authors take objects and show how they differ. Comparison and contrast essays are mostly written in nonfiction form. There are common words used when authors compare or contrast. The list below will show you some of these words:

Comparison Words:

- Similar to
- Alike
- As well as
- Both

Contrast Words:

- Although
- On the other hand
- Different from
- However
- As opposed to
- More than
- Less than

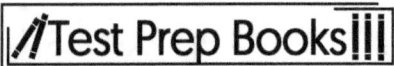

- On the contrary

Cause and Effect
Cause and effect is a common writing device. A cause is why something happens. An effect is what happens because of the cause. Many times, authors use key words to show cause and effect, such as *because, so, therefore, without, now, then,* and *since*. For example: "Because of the sun shower, a rainbow appeared." In this sentence, due to the sun shower (the cause), a rainbow appeared (the effect).

Analogy
An analogy is a comparison between two things. Sometimes the two things are very different from one another. Authors often use analogies to add meaning and make ideas relatable in texts. There are two types of analogies: literal and figurative. A literal analogy compares two objects that are similar in the literal sense. For example, "a kitten is to a cat as a puppy is to a dog". The two concepts (kittens and puppies; cats and dogs) are different, but they are comparable in the sense that both are a younger and older name for an animal. A figurative analogy compares two things that aren't similar in the literal sense. For example, "life is like a race". Life isn't like a literal race, but they both share some common similarities.

Point of View
Point of view is the viewpoint in which authors tell stories. Authors can tell stories in either the first or third person. If an author writes in the first person, they are a character within a story telling about their own experiences. The pronouns *I* and *we* are used when writing in the first person. If an author writes in the third person, the narrator is telling the story from an outside perspective. The author is not a character in the story, but rather tells about the characters' actions and dialogues. Pronouns such as *he, she, it,* and *they* are used in texts written in the third person.

Transitional Words and Phrases
There are approximately 200 transitional words and phrases that are commonly used in the English language. Below are lists of common transition words and phrases.

Time	Example	Compare	Contrast	Addition	Logical Relationships	Steps
after	for example	likewise	however	and	if	first
before	in fact	also	yet	also	then	second
during	for instance		but	furthermore	therefore	last
in the middle				moreover	as a result	
					since	

Transitional words and phrases connect sentences and paragraphs and help a piece of writing make more sense. They provide clearer meaning to readers and a smoother flow to the writing.

Fiction

Fiction is imaginative text that is invented by the author. Fiction is characterized by the following literary elements:

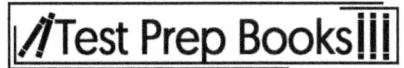

- Characters: the people, animals, aliens, or other living figures the story is about
- Setting: the location, surroundings, and time the story takes place in
- Conflict: a problem that the characters face either internally or externally
- Plot: the sequence and the rise and fall of excitement in the action of a story
- Resolution: the solution to the conflict that is discovered as a result of the story
- Point of View: the lens through which the reader experiences the story
- Theme: the moral to the story or the message the author is sending to the reader

Historical Fiction

Historical fiction is a story that occurs in the past. It uses real settings and characters. Historical fiction can have true events mixed in with events that are made up.

Science Fiction

Science fiction is an invented story. It occurs in the future or in a different world. It often deals with space, time travel, robots, or aliens. It sometimes has highly advanced technology.

Fantasy

Fantasy involves magic or supernatural elements. It can take place in an imaginary world. Examples include talking animals, superheroes rescuing the day, or characters taking on a mythical journey or quest.

Mystery and Adventure

Mystery fiction is a story that involves a puzzle or crime to be solved by the main characters. The mystery is driven by suspense. The reader must sort through clues and distractions to solve the puzzle with the main character. Adventure stories are driven by the risky or exciting action that happens in the plot.

Realistic and Contemporary Fiction

Realistic fiction is when the author shows the world within the story without question. The characters are ordinary. The action could happen in real life. The conflict often involves growing up, family life, or learning to cope with emotion.

Nonfiction Literature

Nonfiction writing is true in detail. Nonfiction can cover almost any topic in the natural world. Nonfiction writers do research and gather facts before writing. Nonfiction has the following subgenres (or subcategories):

Informational text: This is written to tell information to the reader. It may have charts, graphs, indexes, glossaries, or bibliographies.

Persuasive text: This is meant to sway the reader to have a certain opinion or to take action.

Biographies and Autobiographies: Biographies tell details of someone's life. If an author writes the text about someone else, it is a biography. If the author writes it about them self, it is an autobiography.

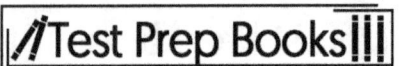

Communicative text: This is used for the purpose of communicating with another person. This includes emails, formal and informal letters, and tweets. This content often consists of two-sided chats between people.

Drama

Drama is any writing that is meant to be performed in front of an audience, such as plays, TV, and movie scripts.

Comedy: Comedy is any drama designed to be funny or lighthearted.

Tragedy: Tragedy is any drama designed to be serious or sad.

Poetry

Poetry is written in verse and often has rhythm. It often involves descriptive imagery, rhyming stanzas, and a beautiful mastery of language. It is often personal, emotional, and reflective. Poetry is often considered a work of art.

Folklore

Folklore is writing that has been handed down from generation to generation by word of mouth. Folklore is often not based in fact but in fanciful beliefs. Folklore is very important to a culture or custom.

Fairy Tales: These are usually written for children and often carry a moral or universal truth. They are stories written about fairies or other magical creatures.

Fables: Similar to fairy tales, fables are written for children and include tales of supernatural people or animals that speak like people.

Myths: Myths are often about the gods, include symbolism, and may involve historical events and reveal human behavior. Sometimes they tell how historical things came about.

Legends: Exaggerated and only partially truthful, these are tales of heroes and important events.

Tall Tales: Often funny stories and sometimes set in the Wild West, these are tales that contain extreme exaggeration.

Interpreting Words and Phrases

Words can have different meanings depending on how they are used in a text. Once a reader knows the correct meaning and how to say a word, they can better understand the context of the word. There are lots of methods for helping readers solve word meanings.

Dictionary: Dictionaries are not allowed on the test. However, readers should know how to use a dictionary and a thesaurus. In dictionaries, there can be more than one meaning for a certain word. Dictionaries also help teach how to say words. A thesaurus teaches words that have the same meanings (synonyms) and words that have opposite meanings (antonyms).

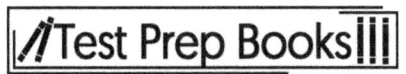

Word Parts: Separating words into their word parts, (root word, prefix, suffix) will help determine the meaning of a word as a whole.

Context Clues: Readers can look at other words in sentences to help them find out the meaning of an unknown word by the way it is used in the same sentence or paragraph. This kind of search provides context clues.

Author's Purpose: Authors use words differently depending on what they want the reader to learn. Some ways writers use words are as follows:

- Literal: the exact meaning of the word
- Figurative: metaphorical language and figures of speech
- Technical: in-depth writing about certain subjects like math or music
- Connotative: showing an opinion in the text as a secondary meaning

Determining Text Structures

Text structures are used for different reasons in writing. Each text structure has key words and elements that help identify it. Readers use text structure to help find information within a text. Summarizing requires knowledge of the text structure of a piece of writing. Here are some common text structures:

Chronological Order: Time order or sequence from one point to another. Dates and times might be used, or bullets and numbering. Possible key words: *first, next, then, after, later, finally, before, preceding, following*

Cause and Effect: Showing how causes lead to effects. Possible key words: *cause, effect, consequently, as a result, due to, in order to, because of, therefore, so, leads to, if/then*

Problem and Solution: Talks about a problem in detail and gives solutions to the problem. Possible key words: *difficulty, problem, solve, solution, possible, therefore, if/then, challenge*

Compare and Contrast: Talks about how objects, people, places, and ideas might be the same or different from each other. Possible key words: *like, unlike, similar to, in contrast, on the other hand, whereas, while, although, either or, opposed to, different from, instead*

Description: Explains a topic with the main idea and details. Possible key words: *for example, such as, for instance, most importantly, another, such as, next to, on top of, besides*

Inference

When readers put together clues from the writing to "guess" that a certain idea is a fact, it is called making inferences. Making inferences helps read "between the lines" of the writing. Readers read "between the lines" to figure out why the author wrote what they wrote.

Inferences are about being able to make wise guesses based on clues from the writing. People make inferences about the world around them every day. However, they may not be aware of what they are doing. For example, a young boy may infer that it is cold outside if he wakes up and his bedroom is chilly. Or, a girl is driving somewhere and she sees a person on the side of the road with a parked car. The girl might think that person's car broke down, and that they are waiting for help. Both of these are examples of how inferences are used every day.

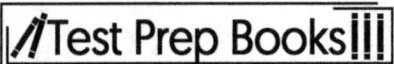

Making inferences is kind of like being a detective. Sometimes clues can be found in the pictures that are inside of a story. For example, a story might show a picture of a school where all the children are in the parking lot. Looking more closely, readers might spot a fire truck parked at the side of the road and might infer that the school had a fire drill or an actual fire.

Summarizing

Readers can summarize writing to find out the main idea in a passage. This helps readers remember what they read and retell the main idea in their own words. Summarizing can sometimes be hard to do. Summarizing means figuring out what's most important in the passage and getting rid of the words that are not important. Summarizing also means taking the first passage and making it smaller. Summarizing uses many of the reader's skills.

Practice Quiz

Read the following passage, and then answer questions 1-2.

> While scientists aren't entirely certain why tornadoes form, they have some clues about the process. Tornadoes are dangerous funnel clouds that occur during a large thunderstorm. When warm, humid air near the ground meets cold, dry air from above, a column of the warm air can be drawn up into the clouds. Winds at different altitudes blowing at different speeds make the column of air rotate. As the spinning column of air picks up speed, a funnel cloud is formed. This funnel cloud moves rapidly and haphazardly. Rain and hail inside the cloud cause it to touch down, creating a tornado. Tornadoes move in a rapid and unpredictable pattern, making them extremely destructive and dangerous. Scientists continue to study tornadoes to improve radar detection and warning times.

1. What is the main purpose of this passage?
    a. Show why tornadoes are dangerous.
    b. Explain how a tornado forms.
    c. Compare thunderstorms to tornadoes.
    d. Explain what to do in the event of a tornado.
    e. Teach readers about the weather.

2. According to the passage why are tornadoes destructive and dangerous?
    a. They are difficult for scientists to study.
    b. They occur during thunderstorms.
    c. They create a spinning column of air.
    d. They move in a rapid and unpredictable pattern.
    e. They improve radar detection and warning times.

Read the following passage, and then answer questions 3-5.

> Vacationers looking for a perfect experience should opt out of Disney parks and try a trip on Disney Cruise Lines. While a park offers rides, characters, and show experiences, it also includes long lines, often very hot weather, and enormous crowds. A Disney cruise, on the other hand, is a relaxing, luxurious vacation that includes many of the same experiences as the parks, minus the crowds and lines. The cruise has top-notch food, maid service, water slides, multiple pools, Broadway-quality shows, and daily character experiences for kids. There are also many activities, such as bingo, trivia contests, and dance parties that can entertain guests of all ages. The cruise even stops at Disney's private island for a beach barbecue with characters, water slides, and water sports. Those looking for the Disney experience without the hassle should book a Disney cruise.

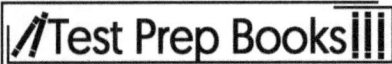

Reading Section

3. What is the main purpose of this passage?
    a. Explain how to book a Disney cruise.
    b. Show what Disney parks have to offer.
    c. Show why Disney parks are expensive.
    d. Compare Disney parks to the Disney cruise.
    e. Entertain readers with an enjoyable story.

4. Which of the following is NOT one of the reasons the author says that Disney cruises are a better option for vacationers than Disney parks?
    a. A Disney cruise is relaxing.
    b. A Disney cruise doesn't make stops.
    c. A Disney cruise has good food.
    d. A Disney cruise has activities that can entertain guests of all ages.
    e. A Disney cruise doesn't have big crowds and lines.

5. What type of passage is this?
    a. Narrative
    b. Informative
    c. Nonfiction
    d. Folklore
    e. Persuasive

See answers on the next page.

Answer Explanations

1. B: The main point of this passage is to show how a tornado forms. Choice *A* is off base because while the passage does mention that tornadoes are dangerous, it is not the main focus of the passage. While thunderstorms are mentioned, they are not compared to tornadoes, so Choice *C* is incorrect. Choice *D* is incorrect because the passage does not discuss what to do in the event of a tornado. Choice *E* is incorrect because it is too broad. The passage is not about weather in general, but is specifically about tornadoes.

2. D: The passage directly states that tornadoes move in a rapid and unpredictable pattern, making them extremely destructive and dangerous.

3. D: The passage compares Disney cruises with Disney parks. It does not discuss how to book a cruise, so Choice *A* is incorrect. Choice *B* is incorrect because, though the passage does mention some of the park attractions, it is not the main point. The passage does not mention the cost of either option, so Choice *C* is incorrect. It is not a story designed to entertain readers; instead, it is an opinion piece, so Choice *E* is incorrect.

4. B: The passage makes note of the benefits listed in Choices *A, C, D,* and *E*. However, Choice *B* states that the cruise doesn't make stops. This is not true. According to the author of the passage, "The cruise even stops at Disney's private island for a beach barbecue with characters, waterslides, and water sports."

5. E: This is a persuasive piece. The author is sharing their opinion and making an argument about why Disney cruises make for a better vacation than Disney parks.

Writing Sample

Test takers are given fifteen minutes to write a story about a picture that is provided. While this section is not scored, the writing sample is provided with the score report to each receiving school. This section gives test takers the opportunity to show their writing ability as well as show creativity and self-expression. Test takers should be sure that their stories have a beginning, a middle, and an end.

Planning should take place after looking at the picture or reading the prompt. This brainstorming stage is when writers consider their purpose and think of ideas that they can use in their writing. Drawing pictures like story webs are great tools to use during the planning stage. Drawing pictures can help connect the writing purpose to supporting details. They can also help begin the process of structuring the writing.

POWER Strategy for Writing

The POWER strategy helps all writers focus and do well during the writing process.

The POWER strategy stands for the following:

- Prewriting or Planning
- Organizing
- Writing a first draft
- Editing the writing
- Revising and rewriting

Prewriting and Planning
During the prewriting and planning phase, writers learn to think about their audience and purpose for the writing assignment. Then they gather information they wish to include in the writing. They do this from their background knowledge or new sources.

Organizing
Next, writers decide on the organization of their writing project. There are many types of organizational structures, but the common ones are: story/narrative, informative, opinion, persuasive, compare and contrast, explanatory, and problem/solution formats.

Writing
In this step, the writers write a first draft of their project.

Evaluating
In this stage, writers reread the writing and note the sections that are strong or that need improvement.

Revising and Rewriting
Finally, the writer incorporates any changes they wish to make based on what they've read. Then writers rewrite the piece into a final draft.

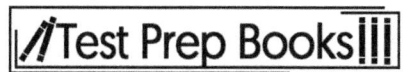

Elements of Effective Writing

The following are characteristics that make writing readable and effective:

- Ideas
- Organization
- Voice
- Word choice
- Sentence fluency
- Proper Writing Conventions
- Presentation

Ideas
This refers to the content of the writing. Writers should focus on the topic shown in the picture or prompt. Then they learn to develop the idea and choose the details that best shows the idea to others.

Organization
Many writers are inclined to jump into their writing without a clear direction for where it is going. Organization helps plan out the writing so that it's successful. Your writing should have an introduction, a body, and a conclusion.

Introduction (beginning): Writers should invite the reader into their work with a good introduction. They should restate the prompt in their own words so that readers know what they are going to read about.

Body (middle): The body is where the main thoughts and ideas are put together. Thoughtful transitions between ideas and key points help keep readers interested. Writers should create logical and purposeful sequences of ideas.

Conclusion (end): Writers should include a powerful conclusion to their piece that summarizes the information but leaves the reader with something to think about.

Voice
Voice is how the writer uses words and sentence structure to sound like themselves. It shows that the writing is meaningful and that the author cares about it. It is what makes the writing uniquely the author's own. It is how the reader begins to know the author and what they "sound like."

Word Choice
The right word choice helps the author connect with their audience. If the work is narrative, the words tell a story. If the work is descriptive, the words can almost make you taste, touch, and feel what you are reading! If the work is an opinion, the words give new ideas and invite thought. Writers should choose detailed vocabulary and language that is clear and lively.

Sentence Fluency
When sentences are built to fit together and move with one another to create writing that is easy to read aloud, the author has written with fluency. Sentences and paragraphs start and stop in just the right places so that the writing moves well. Sentences should have a lot of different structures and lengths.

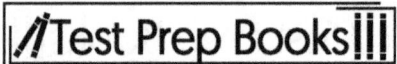

Writing Sample

Proper Writing Conventions

Writers should make their writing clear and understandable through the use of proper grammar, spelling, capitalization, and punctuation.

Presentation

Writers should try to make their work inviting to the reader. Writers show they care about their writing when it is neat and readable.

Tips for the Writing Section

1. Don't panic! This section isn't scored. It is just a great way to show teachers how smart you are and how well you can tell a story and write. You can do it!

2. Use your time well. Fifteen minutes is quick! It is shorter than almost every TV show. Don't spend too much time doing any one thing. Try to brainstorm briefly and then get writing. Leave a few minutes to read it over and correct any spelling mistakes or confusing parts.

3. Be yourself! You are smart and interesting and teachers want to get to know you and your unique ideas. Don't feel pressured to use big vocabulary words if you aren't positive what they mean. You will be more understandable if you use the right word, not the fanciest word.

Practice Writing Sample

Tell a story using the picture below. Make sure that your story has a beginning, middle, and end.

The following pages are provided for writing your story.

Practice Writing Sample

Practice Writing Sample

SSAT Elementary Practice Test #1

Quantitative Section

1. Which of the following is equivalent to the value of the digit 3 in the number 792.134?
    a. 3×1
    b. 3×10
    c. 3×100
    d. $\frac{3}{10}$
    e. $\frac{3}{100}$

2. In the following expression, which operation should be completed first?
$$5 \times 6 + 4 \div 2 - 1$$
    a. Multiplication
    b. Addition
    c. Division
    d. Subtraction
    e. Remainder

3. How would the number 847.89632 be written if rounded to the nearest hundredth?
    a. 847.90
    b. 900
    c. 847.89
    d. 847.896
    e. 800

4. Which of the following is the definition of a prime number?
    a. A number whose only factors are itself and 1
    b. A number greater than 1 whose only factors are itself and 1
    c. A number less than 10
    d. A number divisible by 10
    e. A number that can't be divided by 2

5. What is the next number in the following sequence? 1, 3, 6, 10, 15, 21, ...
    a. 26
    b. 27
    c. 28
    d. 29
    e. 30

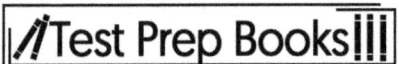

6. Which of the following is the correct order of operations?
   a. Parentheses, Exponents, Multiplication & Division, Addition & Subtraction
   b. Exponents, Parentheses, Multiplication & Division, Addition & Subtraction
   c. Parentheses, Exponents, Addition & Multiplication, Division & Subtraction
   d. Parentheses, Exponents, Division & Addition, Subtraction & Multiplication
   e. Exponents, Parentheses, Addition & Subtraction, Multiplication & Division

7. The perimeter of a six-sided polygon is 56 cm. Three of the sides are each 9 cm long. Two of the other sides are each 8 cm long. What is the length of the missing side?
   a. 10 cm
   b. 11 cm
   c. 12 cm
   d. 13 cm
   e. 14 cm

8. Which of the following is a mixed number?
   a. $16\frac{1}{2}$
   b. 16
   c. $\frac{16}{3}$
   d. $\frac{1}{4}$
   e. 0

9. If you were showing your friend how to round 245.2678 to the nearest thousandth, which place value would be used to decide whether to round up or round down?
   a. Ten-thousandth
   b. Thousandth
   c. Hundredth
   d. Thousands
   e. Hundreds

10. Carey bought 184 pounds of fertilizer to use on her lawn. Each segment of her lawn required $11\frac{1}{2}$ pounds of fertilizer to do a sufficient job. If we are asked to determine how many segments could be fertilized with the amount purchased, what operation would be necessary to solve this problem?
    a. Multiplication
    b. Division
    c. Addition
    d. Subtraction
    e. Exponents

11. It is necessary to line up the decimal places of the numbers before doing which of the following?
    a. Multiplication
    b. Division
    c. Subtraction
    d. Fractions
    e. Exponents

12. Which of the following equations best exemplifies the additive and subtractive identity?
    a. $5 + 1 = 6 + 1 = 7$
    b. $6 + x = 6 - 6$
    c. $9 - 9 = 0$
    d. $8 + 2 = 10$
    e. $5 + 2 - 0 = 5 + 2 + 0$

13. What is an equivalent measurement for 1.3 cm?
    a. 0.13 m
    b. 0.013 m
    c. 0.13 mm
    d. 0.013 mm
    e. 0.0013 mm

14. Katie works at a clothing company and sold 192 shirts over the weekend. One-third of the shirts that were sold were patterned and the rest were solid. Which mathematical expression would calculate the number of solid shirts Katie sold over the weekend?
    a. $192 \times \frac{1}{3}$
    b. $192 \div \frac{1}{3}$
    c. $192 \times (1 - \frac{1}{3})$
    d. $192 \div 3$
    e. $192 - \frac{1}{3}$

15. Which four-sided shape is always a rectangle?
    a. Rhombus
    b. Trapezoid
    c. Parallelogram
    d. Quadrilateral
    e. Square

16. A rectangle was formed out of pipe cleaner. Its length was $\frac{1}{2}$ ft, and its width was $\frac{11}{2}$ inches. What is its area in square inches?
    a. $\frac{11}{4}$ in^2
    b. $\frac{11}{2}$ in^2
    c. 22 in^2
    d. 33 in^2
    e. $\frac{2}{11}$ in^2

17. How would $\frac{4}{5}$ be written as a percent?
   a. 40%
   b. 125%
   c. 90%
   d. 80%
   e. 120%

18. If Danny takes 48 minutes to walk 3 miles, how long should it take him to walk 5 miles maintaining the same speed?
   a. 32 min
   b. 64 min
   c. 80 min
   d. 96 min
   e. 104 min

19. Which of the following represents one hundred eighty-two million, thirty-six thousand, four hundred twenty-one and three hundred fifty-six thousandths?
   a. 182,036,421.356
   b. 182,036,421.0356
   c. 182,000,036,421.0356
   d. 182,000,036,421.356
   e. 182,036,000,421.0356

20. A solution needs 5 mL of saline for every 8 mL of medicine given. How much saline is needed for 45 mL of medicine?
   a. $\frac{225}{8}$ mL
   b. 72 mL
   c. 28 mL
   d. $\frac{45}{8}$ mL
   e. 9 mL

21. What unit is used to describe the volume of the following 3-dimensional shape?

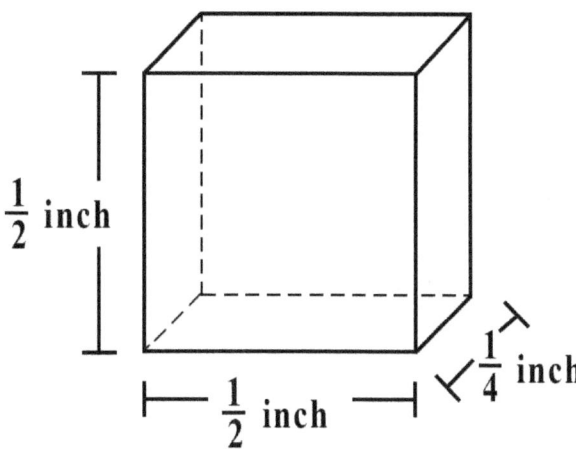

a. Inches
b. Squares
c. Cubics
d. Square inches
e. Cubic inches

22. Which common denominator would be used in order to evaluate $\frac{2}{3} + \frac{4}{5}$?

a. 3
b. 5
c. 8
d. 10
e. 15

23. Which calculation below gives the perimeter of a legal-sized piece of paper that is 14 inches long and $8\frac{1}{2}$ inches wide?

a. $P = 14 + 8\frac{1}{2}$
b. $P = 14 + 8\frac{1}{2} + 14 + 8\frac{1}{2}$
c. $P = 14 \times 8\frac{1}{2}$
d. $P = 14 \times \frac{17}{2}$
e. $P = 14 - \frac{17}{2}$

24. Which of the following are units in the metric system?
a. Inches, feet, miles, pounds
b. Millimeters, centimeters, meters, pounds
c. Kilograms, grams, kilometers, meters
d. Teaspoons, tablespoons, ounces
e. Meters, centimeters, inches, grams

25. Which important mathematical property is shown in the following expression?

$$(7 \times 3) \times 2 = 7 \times (3 \times 2)$$

   a. Distributive property
   b. Commutative property
   c. Associative property
   d. Multiplicative inverse
   e. Reciprocal property

26. The diameter of a circle measures 5.75 centimeters. What tool could be used to draw such a circle?
   a. Ruler
   b. Meter stick
   c. Graph paper
   d. Yard stick
   e. Compass

27. A piggy bank contains 12 dollars' worth of nickels. A nickel weighs 5 grams, and the empty piggy bank weighs 1,050 grams. What is the total weight of the full piggy bank?
   a. 1,110 grams
   b. 1,200 grams
   c. 1,250 grams
   d. 2,200 grams
   e. 2,250 grams

28. Last year, the New York City area received approximately $27\frac{3}{4}$ inches of snow. The Denver area received approximately three times as much snow as New York City. How much snow fell in Denver?
   a. 60 inches
   b. $27\frac{1}{4}$ inches
   c. $9\frac{1}{4}$ inches
   d. $83\frac{1}{4}$ inches
   e. 111 inches

29. Which of the following would be an instance in which ordinal numbers are used?
   a. Katie scored a 9 out of 10 on her quiz.
   b. Matthew finished second in the spelling bee.
   c. Jacob missed one day of school last month.
   d. Kim was 5 minutes late to school this morning.
   e. Eduardo read 7 pages more than he needed to.

30. Evaluate $9 \times 9 \div 9 + 9 - 9 \div 9$.
    a. 0
    b. 17
    c. 81
    d. 9
    e. 1

Verbal Section

Synonyms

Each of the questions below has one word, followed by five other words. Please select one answer whose meaning is closest to the word in capital letters.

1. WEARY:
    a. tired
    b. clothing
    c. happy
    d. hot
    e. whiny

2. VAST:
    a. Rapid
    b. Expansive
    c. Small
    d. Ocean
    e. Uniform

3. DEMONSTRATE:
    a. Tell
    b. Show
    c. Build
    d. Complete
    e. Make

4. ORCHARD:
    a. Flower
    b. Fruit
    c. Grove
    d. Peach
    e. Farm

5. TEXTILE:
    a. Fabric
    b. Document
    c. Mural
    d. Ornament
    e. Knit

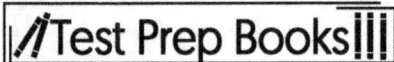

6. OFFSPRING:
    a. Bounce
    b. Parent
    c. Music
    d. Child
    e. Skip

7. PERMIT:
    a. Law
    b. Parking
    c. Crab
    d. Jail
    e. Allow

8. INSPIRE:
    a. Motivate
    b. Impale
    c. Exercise
    d. Patronize
    e. Collaborate

9. WOMAN:
    a. Man
    b. Lady
    c. Women
    d. Girl
    e. Mother

10. ROTATION:
    a. Wheel
    b. Year
    c. Spin
    d. Flip
    e. Orbit

11. CONSISTENT:
    a. Stubborn
    b. Contains
    c. Sticky
    d. Texture
    e. Steady

12. PRINCIPLE:
    a. Principal
    b. Leader
    c. President
    d. Foundation
    e. Royal

13. PERIMETER:
    a. Outline
    b. Area
    c. Side
    d. Volume
    e. Inside

14. SYMBOL:
    a. Drum
    b. Music
    c. Clang
    d. Emblem
    e. Text

15. GERMINATE:
    a. Doctor
    b. Sick
    c. Infect
    d. Plants
    e. Grow

Analogies

The questions below ask you to find relationships between words. For each question, select the answer that best completes the meaning of the sentence.

16. Wheel is to truck as:
    a. foot is to body
    b. steering wheel is to car
    c. truck is to road
    d. head is to body
    e. boat is to river

17. Open is to closed as above is to:
    a. shut
    b. on top
    c. next to
    d. beyond
    e. below

18. Cow is to milk as:
    a. horse is to cow
    b. egg is to chicken
    c. chicken is to egg
    d. glass is to milk
    e. milk is to glass

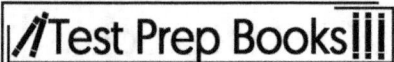

19. Web is to spider as den is to:
    a. living room
    b. eagle
    c. fox
    d. dog
    e. turtle

20. Sad is to blue as happy is to:
    a. glad
    b. yellow
    c. smiling
    d. laugh
    e. calm

21. Door is to store as deal is to:
    a. money
    b. purchase
    c. sell
    d. wheel
    e. market

22. Dog is to veterinarian as baby is to
    a. daycare
    b. mother
    c. puppy
    d. babysitter
    e. pediatrician

23. Clock is to time as:
    a. ruler is to length
    b. jet is to speed
    c. alarm is to sleep
    d. drum is to beat
    e. watch is to wrist

24. Ice is to slippery as rug is to:
    a. soft
    b. carpet
    c. floor
    d. hard
    e. mop

25. Calf is to cow as foal is to:
    a. gerbil
    b. monkey
    c. horse
    d. goat
    e. sheep

26. Wire is to electricity as:
    a. power is to lamp
    b. pipe is to water
    c. fire is to heat
    d. heat is to fire
    e. water is to pipe

27. Currency is to money as:
    a. paper is to plastic
    b. rich is to poor
    c. dollars are to cents
    d. length is to width
    e. story is to tale

28. Cat is to paws as
    a. giraffe is to neck
    b. elephant is to ears
    c. horse is to hooves
    d. snake is to skin
    e. chicken is to feathers

29. Falcon is to mice as giraffe is to
    a. leaves
    b. rocks
    c. antelope
    d. grasslands
    e. neck

30. Executive branch is to president as Judicial Branch is to
    a. Supreme Court Justice
    b. judge
    c. senator
    d. lawyer
    e. congressmen

Reading Section

Read the following passage, and then answer questions 1-4.

Do you want to vacation at a Caribbean island destination? Who wouldn't want a tropical vacation? Visit one of the many Caribbean islands where visitors can swim in crystal blue waters, swim with dolphins, or enjoy family-friendly resorts and activities. Every island offers a unique and dazzling vacation destination. Choose from these islands: Aruba, St. Lucia, Barbados, Anguilla, St. John, and so many more. A Caribbean island destination will be the best and most refreshing vacation ever ... no regrets!

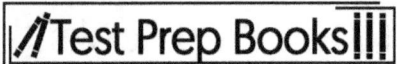

SSAT Elementary Practice Test #1

1. What is the topic of the passage?
    a. Caribbean island destinations
    b. Tropical vacations
    c. Resorts
    d. Activities
    e. Travel

2. What is/are the supporting detail(s) of this passage?
    a. Cruising to the Caribbean
    b. Local events
    c. Family activities
    d. Transportation
    e. All of the above

Read the following sentence, and answer the question below.

"A Caribbean island destination will be the best and most refreshing vacation ever ... no regrets!"

3. What is this sentence an example of?
    a. Imagery
    b. Device
    c. Fallacy
    d. Fact
    e. Opinion

4. What is the author's purpose of this passage?
    a. Entertain readers
    b. Persuade readers
    c. Inform or teach readers
    d. Share a moral lesson to readers
    e. Warn readers

Read the following passage, and then answer questions 5-8.

Even though the rain can put a damper on the day, it can be helpful and fun, too. For one, the rain helps plants grow. Without rain, grass, flowers, and trees would be deprived of vital nutrients they need to develop. Not only does the rain help plants grow, but on days where there are brief spurts of sunshine, rainbows can appear. The rain reflects and refracts the light, creating beautiful rainbows in the sky. Finally, puddle jumping is another fun activity that can be done in or after the rain. Therefore, the rain can be helpful and fun.

5. What is the *cause* in this passage?
    a. Plants growing
    b. Rainbows
    c. Puddle jumping
    d. Rain
    e. Having fun

Read the following sentence, and answer the question below.

> "Without rain, grass, flowers, and trees would be deprived of vital nutrients they need to develop."

6. In this sentence, the author is using what literary device regarding the grass, flowers, and trees?
    a. Comparing
    b. Contrasting
    c. Describing
    d. Transitioning
    e. Simile

7. In the same sentence from above, what is most likely the meaning of *vital*?
    a. Energetic
    b. Truthful
    c. Necessary
    d. Dangerous
    e. Common

8. What is an *effect* in this passage?
    a. Rain
    b. Brief spurts of sunshine
    c. Rainbows
    d. Weather
    e. Temperature

Read the following passage, and then answer questions 9-12.

Lola: The Siberian Husky

Meet Lola ... Lola is an overly friendly Siberian husky who loves her long walks, digs holes for days, and sheds unbelievably ... like a typical Siberian husky. Lola has to be brushed and brushed and brushed—did I mention that she has to be brushed ... all the time! On her long walks, Lola loves making friends with new dogs and kids. A robber could break into our house, and even though they may be intimidated by Lola's wolf-like appearance, the robber would be shocked to learn that Lola would most likely greet them with kisses and a tail wag ... she makes friends with everyone! Out of all the dogs we've ever owned, Lola is certainly one of a kind in many ways.

9. Based on the passage, what does the author imply?
    a. Siberian huskies are great pets, but they require a lot of time and energy.
    b. Siberian huskies are easy to take care of.
    c. Siberian huskies should not be around children.
    d. Siberian huskies are good guard dogs.
    e. Siberian huskies do not usually shed.

10. What word best describes the author of this passage because of their own experience with Siberian huskies?
   a. Impartial
   b. Hasty
   c. Biased
   d. Irrational
   e. Anxious

11. Based on the passage, we can infer what about Lola's owner (the narrator)?
   a. It is a man.
   b. It is a woman.
   c. It is a young child.
   d. It is a new dog owner.
   e. It is an experienced dog owner.

12. Based on the information in the passage, which of the following dogs most likely looks like Lola?
   a.

   b.

   c.

   d.

   e.

Read the following passage, and then answer questions 13-16.

> Learning how to write a ten-minute play may seem like a challenging task at first; but, if you follow a simple creative writing strategy, similar to writing a story, you will be able to write a successful drama. The first step is to open your story as if it is a puzzle to be solved. This will allow the reader to engage with the story and to solve the story with you, the author. Immediately provide descriptive details that set the main idea, the tone, and the mood according to the theme you have in mind. Next, use dialogue to reveal the attitudes and personalities of each of the characters who have a key part in the unfolding story. Show images on stage to speed up the dialogue; remember, one picture speaks a thousand words. As the play progresses, the protagonist must cross the point of no return in some way; this is the climax of the story. Then, as in a written story, you create a resolution to the life-changing event of the protagonist.

13. Based on the passage above, select the statement that is true.
    a. Writing a ten-minute play is very difficult.
    b. Providing descriptive details is not necessary.
    c. The climax of the story sets the theme you have in mind.
    d. Descriptive details give clues to the play's intended mood and tone.
    e. The protagonist is the writer of a ten-minute play.

14. Which of the following is the most likely meaning for the phrase "one picture speaks a thousand words" in the following sentence?

    "Show images on stage to speed up the dialogue; remember, one picture speaks a thousand words."

    a. Audio-video technology should be used to enhance scenery in a play.
    b. Playwrights should be sure to add videos to speed up the dialogue.
    c. Pictures can tell stories as well, if not better, than words.
    d. Playwrights should include an image after every 1000 words of dialogue.
    e. Playwrights should ask actors to speak quickly during images.

15. What is the meaning of the word *protagonist*?
    a. Main character
    b. Actor
    c. Student
    d. Playwright
    e. Teacher

16. In the passage above, the writer suggests that writing a ten-minute play is doable for a new playwright for which of the following reasons?

    a. It took the author of the passage only one week to write their first play.
    b. The format follows strategies similar to those for writing a narrative story.
    c. There are no particular themes or points to unravel in a ten-minute play.
    d. Dialogue is not necessary if you have images.
    e. There is no need to have a climax, so they are easier to create.

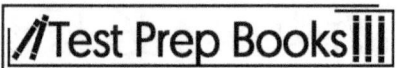

Read the following passage, and then answer questions 17-20.

Overall, we won the Little League championship game! Max hit a winning home run, and we all cheered as he rounded home plate. It was an astonishing win because the other team wins every year and we were down the whole game until the final inning. Our team hoisted the championship trophy up into the air and celebrated with joy. It was such a great game. After the game, my coach took my whole team to the diner and we got burgers, fries, and chocolate milkshakes. Max got grilled cheese because he is a vegetarian. This was the first championship game that our team has won in twenty years. My coach gave a speech while we were eating and said he was proud of our perseverance.

17. What is mostly likely the meaning of *astonishing* in the following sentence?

"It was an astonishing win because the other team wins every year and we were down the whole game until the final inning."

    a. Expected
    b. Surprising
    c. Celebrated
    d. Close
    e. Eager

18. What is the main topic of the passage?
    a. A meal at the diner with his team
    b. A basketball team's victory
    c. Winning the baseball championship
    d. Vegetarian food options at a diner
    e. The baseball coach's speech

19. Which of the following is the best description of the tone or mood of the passage?
    a. Excited
    b. Nervous
    c. Disappointed
    d. Informational
    e. Frustrated

20. Which of the following can readers infer about Max?
    a. He is the narrator of the passage.
    b. He has been on the team for twenty years.
    c. He is overweight.
    d. He does not eat bacon.
    e. He is disappointed.

Read the following passage, and then answer questions 21-24.

When renovating a home, there are several ways to save money. In order to keep a project cost effective, "Do It Yourself," otherwise known as "DIY," projects help put money back into the homeowner's pocket. For example, instead of hiring a contractor to do the demo, rent a dumpster and do the demolition yourself. Another way to keep a home renovation cost effective is to compare prices for goods and services. Many contractors or distributors will match prices from competitors. Finally, if renovating a kitchen or bathroom, leave the layout of the plumbing and electrical the same. Once the process of moving pipes and wires is started, dollars start adding up. Overall, home renovations can be a pricey investment, but there are many ways to keep project costs down.

21. Which of the following statements is true based on the information in the passage?
    a. Home improvement projects can be expensive, but there are ways to keep costs down.
    b. Home renovations require a lot of work, which is why a contractor should be hired to complete the job.
    c. It is not necessary for homeowners to compare prices of contractors because they are their own best bet.
    d. Many contractors and distributors charge more than competitors for goods and services.
    e. DIY projects are more costly than hiring a professional, but are easy to do.

22. What is the meaning of the following sentence? "Do It Yourself," otherwise known as "DIY," projects help put money back into the homeowner's pocket.
    a. Homeowners get paid to do their own renovations.
    b. Homeowners will find money in their house while they are doing repairs.
    c. Hiring a contractor is more cost-effective than doing your own repairs.
    d. Homeowners save money by doing home repairs themselves.
    e. Homeowners get a rebate for doing repairs.

23. Based on the opinion of the author, readers can infer that the author is likely which of the following?
    a. Someone who is a contractor
    b. Someone who is a distributor
    c. Someone who is very rich
    d. Someone who likes deals
    e. Someone who sells hardware

24. Which of the following correctly lists the ways to keep renovation costs down, according to the author?
    a. Rent a dumpster, compare prices for goods and services, keep the layout of plumbing and electric.
    b. Rent a dumpster, compare prices for goods and services, change the pipes and wires.
    c. Hire a contractor for the demolition, compare prices for goods and services, keep the layout of plumbing and electric.
    d. Hire a contractor for the demolition, compare prices for goods and services, change the pipes and wires.
    e. Hire a contractor for the demolition, rent a dumpster, change the pipes and wires.

Read the following poem, and then answer questions 25-28.

Standing in front of the mirror, I like to look at my face
I smile and frown and laugh and scream, emotions all over the place
Sometimes I stand between my mom and dad, all three of us in a row
We look each other up and down from the tops of our heads to the tips of our toes

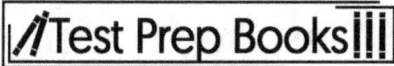

My mom says I have her nose and her ears and a smile just like my dad
Our shirts and pants look different though because I wear jeans and dad wears plaid
Our hair color is also different though, which is confusing to me
Dad has black, mom has blond, but mine is brown like the bark of a tree
My teacher told me we inherit genes from our parents that affect how we look and act
Some of our features look like one or both of them, while some are unique to us in fact.
I am glad that I carry parts of mom and dad on my face and in my heart
That way they are with me wherever I go, even when we are apart.

25. Which of the following pairs of words in the poem are homophones?
    a. Fact and act
    b. Genes and jeans
    c. Plaid and dad
    d. Mirror and inherit
    e. Blond and bark

26. Which of the following lines most likely was meant to have a figurative, not literal, meaning?
    a. My mom says I have her nose and her ears.
    b. We look each other up and down.
    c. My teacher told me we inherit genes from our parents that affect how we look and act.
    d. Standing in front of the mirror, I like to look at my face.
    e. Our hair color is also different though, which is confusing to me.

27. What does this poem teach readers?
    a. Children tend to look like people they are related to.
    b. If your hair color is brown, you don't look like your parents.
    c. Children and parents wear different types of pants.
    d. You should carry a mirror with you wherever you go.
    e. Children and parents are identical.

28. Which of the following is likely not an inherited trait?
    a. Facial features
    b. Genes
    c. Jeans
    d. Behavior
    e. Emotions

SSAT Elementary Practice Test #1

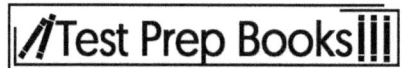

Writing Sample

Tell a story using the picture below. Make sure that your story has a beginning, middle, and end.

The following pages are provided for writing your story.

Answer Explanations

Quantitative Section

1. E: Digits to the left of the decimal point represent the digit value times increasing multiples of 10 (first 1, then 10, 100, 1,000, and so on). Digits to the right of the decimal point represent the digit value divided by increasing multiples of 10 (first $\frac{1}{10}$, then $\frac{1}{100}$, $\frac{1}{1000}$, and so on). So, the second digit to the right of the decimal point equals the digit value divided by 100.

2. A: Using the order of operations, multiplication and division are computed first from left to right. Multiplication is on the left; therefore, multiplication should be performed first.

3. A: The hundredths place value is located two digits to the right of the decimal point (the digit 9 in the original number). To decide whether to round up or keep the digit, examine the digit to the right, and if it is 5 or greater, round up. In this case, the digit to the right is 6, so the hundredths place is rounded up. When rounding up, if the digit to be increased is a 9, the digit to its left is increased by one, and the digit in the desired place value is made a zero. Therefore, the number is rounded to 847.90.

4. B: A prime number is a number whose only factors are itself and 1, but only numbers greater than 1 can be considered prime.

5. C: Starting with 1, we get the next number in the sequence by adding 2, then 3, 4, 5, and 6. So to find the next number, we take our latest number and add 7, getting $21 + 7 = 28$.

6. A: Order of operations follows PEMDAS: Parentheses, Exponents, Multiplication and Division from left to right, and Addition and Subtraction from left to right.

7. D. The perimeter is found by calculating the sum of all sides of the polygon:

$$9 + 9 + 9 + 8 + 8 + s = 56$$

Let s be the missing side length. Therefore, $43 + s = 56$. The missing side length is 13 cm.

8. A: A mixed number contains both a whole number and a fraction.

9. A: We use the place value to the right of the thousandths place, which would be the ten-thousandths place. The value in the thousandths place is 7. The number in the place value to its right is greater than 4, so the 7 is bumped up to 8. Everything to its right is removed, which gives us 245.268.

10. B: This is a division problem because the original amount needs to be split up into equal amounts. Although it's not required to answer the test question, we could solve Carey's problem as follows. The mixed number $11\frac{1}{2}$ should be converted to an improper fraction first:

$$11\frac{1}{2} = \frac{(11 \times 2) + 1}{2} = \frac{23}{2}$$

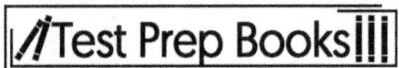

Answer Explanations

Carey needs to determine how many times $\frac{23}{2}$ goes into 184. This is a division problem:

$$184 \div \frac{23}{2} = ?$$

The fraction can be flipped, and the problem turns into multiplication:

$$184 \times \frac{2}{23} = \frac{368}{23}$$

This improper fraction can be simplified into 16 because $368 \div 23 = 16$. The answer is 16 lawn segments.

11. C: Numbers should be lined up by decimal places before subtraction is performed. Subtraction only works when the place value on top is the same as on the bottom. With the other operations—multiplying, dividing, and calculating exponents (which is a form of multiplication)—we ignore the decimal places at first and then include them at the end.

12. E: The additive and subtractive identity is zero. When added to or subtracted from any number, zero does not change the original number.

13. B: 100 cm is equal to 1 m. 1.3 divided by 100 is 0.013. Therefore, 1.3 cm is equal to 0.013 m. Because 1 cm is equal to 10 mm, 1.3 cm is equal to 0.013 m.

14. C: $\frac{1}{3}$ of the shirts sold were patterned. Therefore, $1 - \frac{1}{3}$ (that is, $\frac{2}{3}$) of the shirts sold were solid. A fraction of something is calculated with multiplication, so $192 \times (1 - \frac{1}{3})$ solid shirts were sold. (We could calculate that this equals 128, but that's not necessary for this question.)

15. E: A rectangle is a specific type of parallelogram. It has 4 right angles. A square is a rhombus that has 4 right angles. Therefore, a square is always a rectangle because it has two sets of parallel lines and 4 right angles.

16. D: Recall the formula for area of a rectangle, $area = length \times width$. The answer must be in square inches, so all values must be converted to inches. Half of a foot is equal to 6 inches. Therefore, the area of the rectangle is equal to:

$$6 \text{ in} \times \frac{11}{2} \text{ in} = \frac{66}{2} \text{ in}^2 = 33 \text{ in}^2$$

17. D: To convert a fraction to a percent, we can first convert the fraction to a decimal. To do so, divide the numerator by the denominator: $4 \div 5 = 0.8$. To convert a decimal to a percent, multiply by 100: $0.8 \times 10 = 80\%$.

18. C: To solve the problem, we can write a proportion consisting of ratios comparing distance and time. One way to set up the proportion is:

$$\frac{3}{48} = \frac{5}{x}$$

Answer Explanations

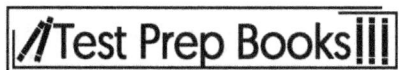

To solve this proportion, we can cross-multiply:

$$(3)(x) = (5)(48) \text{ or } 3x = 240$$

To isolate the variable, we divide by 3 on both sides, producing $x = 80$.

19. A: 182 is in the millions, 36 is in the thousands, and 421 is in the ones. After the decimal point, 356 is positioned with its last digit in the thousandths place (the third digit).

20. A: Every 8 mL of medicine requires 5 mL of saline. The 45 mL first needs to be split into portions of 8 mL. This results in $\frac{45}{8}$ portions. Each portion requires 5 mL of saline. Therefore:

$$\frac{45}{8} \times 5 = \frac{225}{8} \text{ mL is necessary.}$$

21. E: The volume of this 3-dimensional figure is calculated using length times width times height. Each of these three measurements is in inches. Therefore, the answer would be labeled in cubic inches.

22. E: A common denominator must be found. The least common denominator is 15 because it has both 5 and 3 as factors. The fractions must be rewritten using 15 as the denominator.

23. B: Perimeter of a rectangle is the sum of all four sides. Therefore, the answer is

$$P = 14 + 8\frac{1}{2} + 14 + 8\frac{1}{2} = 45 \text{ square inches}$$

24. C: Variants of "gram" (including kilograms) and variants of "meter" (including kilometers, centimeters, and millimeters) belong to the metric system. The other units listed above are not all part of the metric system.

25. C: It shows the associative property of multiplication. The order of multiplication does not matter, and the grouping symbols do not change the final result once the expression is evaluated.

26. E: A compass is a tool that can be used to draw a circle. The other tools could not effectively be used to draw a circle.

27. E: A dollar contains 20 nickels. Therefore, if there are 12 dollars' worth of nickels, there are $12 \times 20 = 240$ nickels. Each nickel weighs 5 grams. Therefore, the weight of the nickels is:

$$240 \times 5 = 1,200 \text{ grams}$$

To find the total weight of the filled piggy bank, add the weight of the nickels and the weight of the empty bank:

$$1,200 + 1,050 = 2,250 \text{ grams.}$$

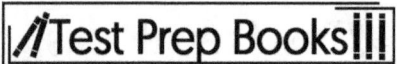

28. D: To find Denver's total snowfall, 3 must be multiplied by $27\frac{3}{4}$. In order to easily do this, the mixed number should be converted into an improper fraction.

$$27\frac{3}{4} = \frac{27 \times 4 + 3}{4} = \frac{111}{4}$$

Therefore, Denver had approximately $\frac{3 \times 111}{4} = \frac{333}{4}$ inches of snow. The improper fraction can be converted back into a mixed number through division.

$$\frac{333}{4} = 83\frac{1}{4} \text{ inches}$$

29. B: Ordinal numbers represent a ranking. Placing second in a competition is a ranking among the other participants of the spelling bee.

30. B: According to order of operations, multiplication and division must be completed first from left to right. Then, addition and subtraction are completed from left to right. Therefore:

$$9 \times 9 \div 9 + 9 - 9 \div 9$$

$$81 \div 9 + 9 - 9 \div 9$$

$$9 + 9 - 1$$

$$18 - 1$$

$$= 17$$

Verbal Section

1. A: Weary most closely means tired. Someone who is weary and tired may be whiny, but they do not necessarily mean the same thing.

2. B: Something that is vast is big and expansive. Choice *D*, ocean, may be described as vast. However, the word itself does not mean vast. The heavens or skies may also be described as vast. Someone's imagination or vocabulary can also be vast.

3. B: To demonstrate something means to show it. A demonstration is a show-and-tell type of example. It is usually visual.

4. C: An orchard is most like a grove. Both are areas like plantations that grow different kinds of fruit. Peach is a type of fruit that may be grown in an orchard. However, *peach* is not a synonym for orchard. Many citrus fruits are grown in groves. But either word can be used to describe many fruit-bearing trees in one area. Choice *E*, farm, may have an orchard or grove on the property. However, they are not the same thing, and many farms do not grow fruit trees.

5. A: *Textile* is another word for fabric. The most confusing choice in this case is Choice *E*, knit. This is because some textiles are knit, but *textile* and *knit* are not synonym. Plenty of textiles are not knit.

6. D: Offspring are the kids of parents. This word is common when talking about the animal kingdom. Though it can be used with humans as well. *Offspring* does have the word *spring* in it. But it has nothing

Answer Explanations

to do with bounce, Choice A. Choice B, parent, maybe tricky because parents have offspring. But for this reason, they are not synonyms.

7. E: Permit can be a verb or a noun. As a verb, it means to allow or give permission for something. As a noun, it refers to a document or something that has been authorized like a parking permit or driving permit. This would allow the authorized person to park or drive under the rules of the document.

8. A: If someone is inspired, they are driven to do something. Someone who is an inspiration motivates others to follow their lead.

9. B: A woman is a lady. You must read carefully and remember the difference between *woman* and *women*. *Woman* refers to one person who is female. *Women* is the plural form and refers to more than one, or a group of ladies. A woman can be a mother, but not necessarily. *Woman* and *mother* are not synonyms. A girl is a child and not yet a woman.

10. C: Rotation means to spin or turn, like a wheel rotating on a car. But *wheel*, Choice A, does not mean the same thing as the word *rotation*.

11. E: Something that is consistent is steady, predictable, reliable, or constant. The tricky one here is that the word *consistency* comes from the word *consistent*. *Consistency* may describe a texture or something that is sticky, Choices C and D. *Consistent* also comes from the word *consist*. Consist means to contain, Choice B. You must know some vocabulary to recognize the differences in these words.

12. D: A principle is a guiding idea or belief. Someone with good moral character is described as having strong principles. You must be careful not to get confused with the homonyms *principle* and *principal*, Choice A. These two words have different meanings. A principal is the leader of a school. The word principal also refers to the main idea or most important thing.

13. A: Perimeter refers to the outline of an object. You may recognize that word from math class. In math class, perimeter refers to the edges or distance around a closed shape. Some of the other choices refer to other math words encountered in geometry. However, they do not have the same meaning as *perimeter*.

14. D: A symbol is an object, picture, or sign that is used to represent something. For example, a pink ribbon is a symbol for breast cancer awareness. A flag can be a symbol for a country. The tricky part of this question was also knowing the meaning of *emblem*. An *emblem* is a design that represents a group or concept, much like a symbol. Emblems often appear on flags or a coat of arms.

15. E: Germinate means to develop or grow. It most often refers to sprouting seeds as a new plant first breaks through the seed coat. It can also refer to the development of an idea. Choice D, *plants*, may be an attractive choice since plants germinate. However, the word *germinate* does not mean *plant*.

16. A: The best fit here is wheel is to truck as foot is to body. Wheels are the part of the truck that make contact with the ground to roll the vehicle forward. Feet are the part of the body that walk on the ground during locomotion.

17. E: Open and closed are opposites, so the question is looking for the opposite of *above*. Choices A (shut), C (next to), and D (beyond) are not opposites. Choice B (on top) is a synonym of above, so it may be tricky but it is not correct. The opposite or antonym for above is *below*.

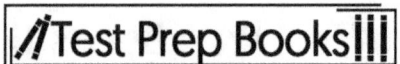

Answer Explanations

18. C: Cows produce milk, so the question is looking for another pair that has a producer and their product. Horses don't produce cows, Choice *A*, glasses don't produce milk, Choice *D*, and milk doesn't produce a glass, Choice *E*. The correct choice is *C*: chicken is to egg. The tricky one here is Choice *B*, egg is to chicken, because it has the correct words but the wrong order; therefore, it reverses the relationship. Eggs don't produce chickens so it does not work with the first part of the analogy: cow is to milk.

19. C: The first part of the analogy – web is to spider – describes the home (web) and who lives in it (spider), so the question is looking for what animal lives in a den. The best choice is *C*, fox. Living room, Choice *A*, is a synonym for a den.

20. A: Sad and blue are synonyms because they both describe the same type of mood. The word *blue* in this case is not referring to the color. Therefore, although Choice *B*, yellow, is sometimes considered a "happy" color, the question isn't referring to blue as a color. Yellow and happy are not synonyms. Someone who is happy may laugh or smile, Choices *C* and *D*. However, these words are not synonyms for happy. Lastly, someone who is happy may be calm, Choice *E*, although they could also be excited. Calm and happy are not synonyms. The best choice is glad.

21. D: The key to answering this question correctly is to recognize the relationship between door and store. Door and store are both words that rhyme. You might be thinking that stores have doors. However, after seeing the other word choices and the given word *deal*, you should notice that none of the other words have this relationship. Instead, the answer should rhyme with *deal*. Wheel and deal, although spelled differently, are rhyming words. Therefore, the correct answer is *D*.

22. E: This question tests your knowledge of jobs. Dogs are taken care of by veterinarians. So the solution is looking for who takes care of babies. However, mothers and babysitters, Choices *B* and *D*, can also take care of babies. Veterinarians take care of sick dogs and act as a medical doctor for pets. Therefore, with this higher level of detail, test takers should select pediatrician. Pediatricians are doctors for babies and children.

23. A: The relationship in the first half of the analogy is that clocks are used to measure time. The second half of the analogy should have a tool that is used to measure something followed by what it measures. Rulers can be used to measure length. So Choice *A* is the best choice. Remember that the key to solving analogies is to be a good detective. Some of the other answer choices are related to clocks and time but not to the relationship between clocks and time.

24. A: *Slippery* is an adjective that describes the surface of ice. The answer is best filled by a word that describes rugs, such as soft, Choice *A*. Carpet, Choice *B*, is a synonym for a rug rather than an adjective that describes rugs. Therefore, that is an incorrect choice. Rugs cover the floor, Choice *C*, so again, this is not an adjective for a rug and not the correct answer. Hard, Choice *D*, is an adjective, but the opposite of describing a rug. Mop, Choice *E*, is not correct, as it does not describe rugs.

25. C: A calf is a baby cow, and a foal is a baby horse. Choice *C* is the only answer choice that makes sense.

26. B: Wires are the medium that carry electricity, allowing the current to flow in a circuit. Pipes carry water in a similar fashion. So the best choice is *B*. You must be careful to not select Choice *E*, water is to pipe. This reverses the relationship between the two. Choices *A*, *C*, and *D* contain words that are related to one another but not in the same way as wires and electricity.

Answer Explanations

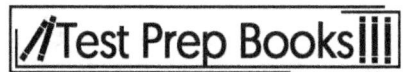

27. E: Currency and money have the same meaning. Currency is a word used to describe the money in a country or region. Therefore, the best choice is *E*. Astor and a tale mean the same thing.

28. C: This is a part/whole analogy. The common thread is what animals walk on. Choices *A*, *B*, and *E* all describe certain parts of animals. However, paws are not the defining feature of cats. While snakes travel on their skin, they do not walk.

29. A: This is a consumer/food analogy. The theme of this analogy is pairing a specific animal to their food source. Falcons prey on mice. Giraffes are herbivores and only eat one of the choices: leaves. Grasslands, Choice *D*, describe a type of landscape, not a food source for animals.

30. A: This question asks you to know the basic roles and positions of the three branches of the government. The president serves in the executive branch, and the Supreme Court justices serve in the judicial branch.

Reading Section

1. A: Caribbean island destinations. The topic of the passage can be described in a one- or two-word phrase. Choices *B*, *C*, and *D* are all mentioned in the passage. However, they are too vague to be considered the main topic of the passage.

2. C: Remember that supporting details help readers find out the main idea by answering questions like *who, what, where, when, why,* and *how*. In this question, cruises and local events are not talked about in the passage. However, family resorts and activities are talked about.

3. E: An opinion is when the author states their own thoughts on a subject. In this sentence, the author says that the reader will not regret the vacation. The author says that it may be the best and most relaxing vacation. But this may not be true for the reader. Therefore, the statement is the author's opinion. Facts would have evidence, like that collected in a science experiment.

4. B: Persuade readers. The author is trying to persuade readers to go to a Caribbean island destination by giving the reader fun facts and a lot of fun options. Not only does the author give a lot of details to support their opinion, the author also implies that the reader would be "wrong" if they didn't want to visit a Caribbean island. This means the author is trying to persuade the reader to visit a Caribbean island.

5. D: Rain is the cause in this passage because it is why something happened. The effects are plants growing, rainbows, and puddle jumping.

6. A: The author is comparing the plants, trees, and flowers. The author is showing how these things react the same to rain. They all get important nutrients from rain. If the author described the differences, then it would be contrasting, Choice *B*.

7. C: *Vital* can mean different things depending on the context or how it is used. But in this sentence, the word *vital* means necessary. The word *vital* means full of life and energy. Choices *A* and *B*, *energetic* and *truthful*, do not make sense. Choice *D*, *dangerous*, is almost an antonym for the word we are looking for since the sentence says the nutrients are needed for growing. Something needed would not be dangerous. Choice *E*, *vigorous*, also does not make sense. The best context clue is that it says the vital nutrients are needed, which tells us they are necessary.

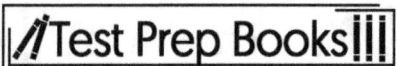

Answer Explanations

8. C: Rainbows. This passage mentions several effects. Effects are the outcome of a certain cause. Remember that the cause here is rain, so Choice *A* is incorrect. Since the cause is rain, Choice *B*—brief spurts of sunshine—doesn't make sense because rain doesn't *cause* brief spurts of sunshine. Choice *C* makes the most sense because the effects of the rain in the passage are plants growing, rainbows, and puddle jumping. Choice *D*, weather, is not an effect of rain but describes rain in a general sense. Lastly, Choice *E*, temperature, is not correct because the passage does not mention the rain causing any changes in temperature.

9. A: The author implies that Siberian huskies are great pets who also require a lot of time and energy. In the passage, the writer describes how huskies require lots of brushing, need long walks, and frequently dig, making them difficult to care for. The author also talks about how friendly Siberian huskies can be, even possibly greeting a robber at their own house, which would definitely make them bad guard dogs.

10. C: Biased: The author may be biased because they show that they like one dog breed over another in an unfair way. Choice *A*, impartial, is the opposite of biased and means very fair, without being opinionated. Hasty, Choice *B*, means quick to judge, and irrational, Choice *D*, means something that doesn't make sense. Choice *E*, anxious, means nervous or worried, and this narrator does not seem nervous or anxious.

11. E: It is an experienced dog owner. We do not have any clues from the paragraph whether the narrator is a man, woman, or young child, so Choices *A*, *B*, and *C* are incorrect. Also, the narrator talks about having other dogs before, so they cannot be a new dog owner. Therefore, Choice *D* is incorrect. Choice *E* makes sense because the narrator talks about having other dogs before Lola, which means that they have been a dog owner before.

12. A: Choice *A* is a photo of a Siberian Husky like Lola. Test takers do not need to be familiar with different dog breeds to correctly answer this question. Instead, they can be detectives and use clues from the passage about what Lola looks like. For one, the narrator mentions Lola's long fur, which sounds bushy and full because it has to be brushed so much! Dogs in Choices *B* and *C* (the Chihuahua and the Dalmatian) are ruled out because of their short hair. The narrator also mentions that Lola has a "wolf-like appearance" that may scare a robber. Even though Choice *D* (a Shih-Tzu) has very long hair, that dog does not look like a wolf. Furthermore, Choices *B*, *C*, and *E* do not look like wolves.

13. D: Readers should focus on the details in the passage to answer this question. The beginning of the passage, as well as the main idea, states that writing ten-minute plays may *seem* difficult, but it actually isn't. Therefore, Choice *A* is incorrect. Choices *B* and *D* are opposites. The passage mentions how descriptive details *are* important to help set the mood, tone, and theme, so Choice *B* is incorrect, and Choice *D* is the best answer. Lastly, it is said that the theme is set in the descriptive details. The theme should come right at the beginning of the play and not the climax, so Choice *C* is incorrect. Protagonists are main characters, not playwrights, so Choice *E* is incorrect.

14. C: Pictures can tell stories as well, if not better, than words. This is a phrase used a lot in the English language. In the case of a ten-minute play, playwrights would be smart to use images to cut down on the dialogue, since ten minutes is not a long time. This passage was all about how writing a short play isn't actually that hard even for a new playwright. The author of the passage persuades readers by stating that pictures make it a lot simpler.

15. A: The protagonist of a story is the main character. Without knowing this, test takers can try to find the correct choice by using clues from the passage. The passage states: *As the play progresses, the*

Answer Explanations

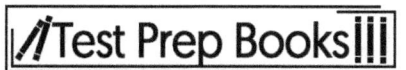

protagonist must cross the point of no return in some way; this is the climax of the story. Then, as in a written story, you create a resolution to the life-changing event of the protagonist. This information should help rule out Choices *C, D,* and *E* (student, playwright, and teacher) since it is clear that the protagonist is in the play. Choice *B*, actor, may be an attractive choice since an actor is in the play, but careful readers will notice that is says *the protagonist* meaning there is only one. There are likely multiple actors in the play, because the passage mentions dialogue, which must include at least two people.

16. B: The passage does not talk about how long a playwright spends doing revisions and rewrites. So, Choice *A* is incorrect. Choice *B* is correct because of the opening statement: "Learning how to write a 10-minute play may seem like a monumental task at first; but, if you follow a simple creative writing strategy, similar to the ones used for writing narrative stories, you will be able to write a successful drama." None of the other choices are supported by points in the passage.

17. B: *Astonishing* most closely means surprising. Choice *A*, expected, can be ruled out because the same sentence mentions that the other team wins every year. Choice *D*, "a close win," does not make sense because the narrator does not say anything about the actual score. Readers may be tempted to choose *celebrated,* Choice *C,* because the passage mentions a lot of celebrating. However, using clues from the sentence that the other team always wins would help make *surprising* a better choice. Choice *E, eager,* does not make any sense because that means excitedly waiting for something.

18. C: The passage talks about Little League and Max scoring the winning run. These are clues that it is about baseball. So, Choice *B* is incorrect. The main idea of the story is about the baseball team winning the championships. It is true that the team eats at the diner, and one player is a vegetarian, and the coach makes a speech. However, these are supporting details.

19. A: This question was a little tricky because both *A* and *D* seem like they could be true. Nervous, disappointed, and frustrated, Choices *B C,* and *E*, should be easy to rule out because the narrator was happy about the win. The passage does mention that the other team usually wins, and it has been twenty years since the narrator's team won. However, these are just details. Choice *D*, informational, is not really a tone or mood. It refers to a type of writing that is educational. This passage is a story with excited emotion.

20. D: Readers are told that Max is a vegetarian. This means he does not eat meat. Bacon is a meat, so we can guess that Max does not eat bacon. Choice *A* is incorrect because the narrator mentions Max by name and doesn't say "I," so the narrator is not Max. We can also infer that Max has not been on the team for twenty years, because he would be too old! Max is also not disappointed, Choice *E,* because his team won and he seems very excited. Readers may be tempted to choose Choice *C*, that Max is overweight, because it mentions that he follows a specific diet (vegetarian). However, he is active and in sports and got the winning run. Therefore, Choice *D* makes more sense than Choice *C.*

21. A: The main idea of the passage is that home improvement projects can be expensive. However, there are ways to keep the costs down. The details of the other choices go against what the passage says. So, they are incorrect. For example, the passage says that contractors will often price-match competitors. This makes Choice *D* incorrect. Choice *B* is incorrect because one of the author's main points is that they do not need to hire a contractor for all renovations. They can do it themselves as a DIY project. Choice *C* is incorrect because the passage does mention that some projects require professionals, but that comparing prices can minimize costs. Choice *E* is incorrect because the main

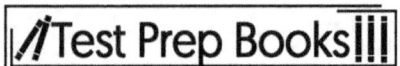

Answer Explanations

point is that many DIY projects are possible and a good way to save money; therefore, they are not more expensive.

22. D: Something that is "like money on your pocket" means that it is money savings or a deal. This is a common phrase. Choice A doesn't make sense, because how would they get paid to do their own repairs? Who would pay them and why? Similarly, while some change may be found in couch cushions or loose money around some people's homes, Choice B, finding money while doing repairs, is not a likely choice. Choice C is incorrect based on the main idea and details mentioned in the passage. For example, readers are encouraged in the passage not to get a contractor to do the demolition, but to rent a dumpster themselves to save money.

23. D: Readers can guess that the author of the passage likes to find deals. For this reason, Choice C is more unlikely than Choice D, because if the narrator was very rich, they may be less interested in strategies to save money. The advice in the passage is mostly doing projects yourself, so the narrator is probably not a distributor, contractor, or hardware salesmen. For this reason, Choices C, D, and E are incorrect.

24. A: Readers must look carefully over the paragraph to find the author's advice. Readers will find that the author of the passage says to rent a dumpster, compare prices for goods and services, and keep the layout of plumbing and electric. The other answer choices had at least one incorrect suggestion.

25. B: Homophones are words that have the same pronunciation but different meanings or spellings. A good example of this is *new* and *knew*. New means something that has only existed for a short period of time. Knew, on the other hand, refers to the past tense of the verb to know, meaning to be aware of something. To answer this question correctly, test takers must be able to properly read the words genes and jeans. Genes are the genetic material that dictate a person's traits. Jeans are denim pants. The other answer choices provided were either pairs of rhyming words or simply two unrelated words.

26. A: My mom says I have her nose and her ears is an example of figurative language. Figurative language describes things using creative and imaginative terms, similes and metaphors, and poetic language. The words do not mean exactly what they say. In this case, the child narrating the poem does not truly have the mom's nose and ears. Those features are stuck on the mom's face! Instead, what is meant is that the child's features look very much like the nose and ears of the mom. This is a poetic expression. This is not a fact that should be taken with a literal meaning. The other choices are examples of lines in the poem with more literal meanings. Literal is when words mean what they say without any sort of imaginative language.

27. A: This poem teaches readers that children often have characteristics that look like their parents. This is because we inherit genes from our parents and these genes have something called DNA, which tells our body what we should look like. The other choices are not really lessons that the poem is teaching readers. Some children with brown hair look like their parents who may also have brown hair. Children and parents may wear different types of pants, but they don't have to. They can wear pants that are very similar. Also, it is not usually necessary to carry a mirror wherever one goes. Lastly, children are not identical to their parents. The poem says they have some similar traits and some unique ones as well.

28. C: Genes are inherited, but jeans are clothing. Blue jeans may be passed down from an older sibling or parent as a hand-me-down. However, they are not a characteristic of an individual. Traits are what a person is as a whole.

SSAT Elementary Practice Test #2

Quantitative Section

1. Which of the following whole numbers is NOT a multiple of 8?
    a. 80
    b. 2
    c. 32
    d. 48
    e. 16

2. Find the value of the following: $233 + 592$.
    a. 725
    b. 835
    c. 815
    d. 925
    e. 825

3. Find the value of $2 + 8 \times 3 - 4 \div 2$.
    a. 13
    b. 24
    c. 26
    d. 18
    e. 5

4. Which of the following is between $\frac{1}{3}$ and $\frac{2}{5}$?
    a. $\frac{1}{4}$
    b. $\frac{2}{3}$
    c. $\frac{6}{7}$
    d. $\frac{1}{2}$
    e. $\frac{3}{8}$

5. Find the sum of 5.67 and 2.3.
    a. 7.97
    b. 7.7
    c. 8.97
    d. 8.7
    e. 8.17

6. Morgan wants to exercise at least 3 hours total this week. He exercised 35 minutes on Monday, 22 minutes on Tuesday, 41 minutes on Wednesday, and 1 hour on Thursday. How many more minutes does Morgan need to exercise to reach his goal of 3 hours?
   a. 39
   b. 81
   c. 25
   d. 44
   e. 22

7. In the following bar graph, how many total children prefer brownies or cake?

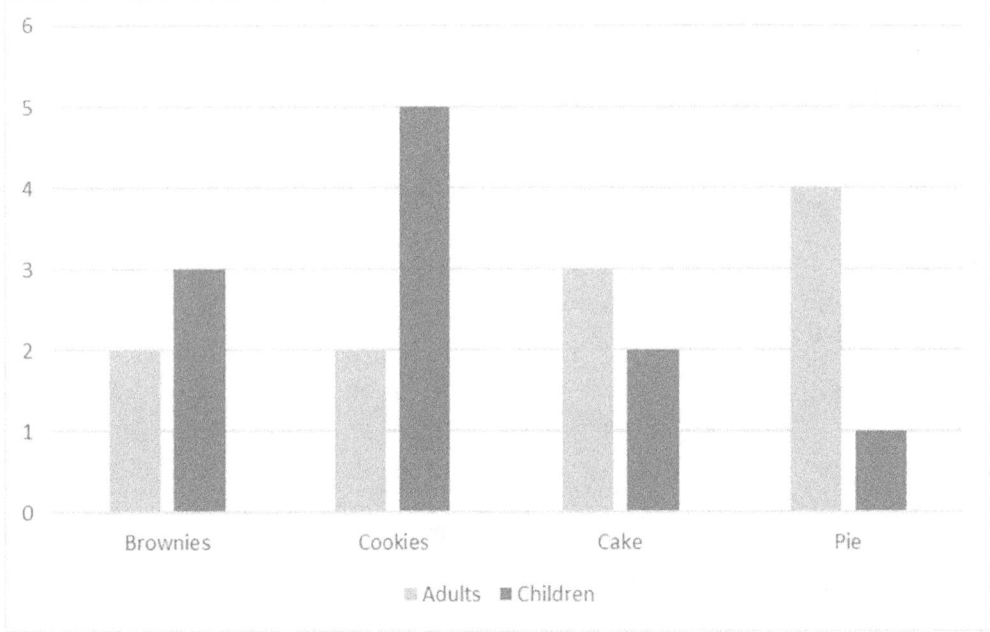

   a. 3
   b. 4
   c. 7
   d. 6
   e. 5

8. Which of the following is represented by $6,000 + 400 + 30 + 5$?
   a. 5,346
   b. 6,345
   c. 64,305
   d. 6,435
   e. 53,460

9. What method is used to convert a fraction to a decimal?
   a. Divide the denominator by the numerator.
   b. Multiply by 100 and reduce the fraction.
   c. Divide the numerator by the denominator.
   d. Divide by 100 and reduce the fraction.
   e. Multiply by 10 and reduce the fraction.

10. In Jim's school, there are a total of 650 students. There are three girls for every two boys. How many students are girls?
    a. 260 girls
    b. 130 girls
    c. 65 girls
    d. 390 girls
    e. 325 girls

11. When evaluating word problems, which of the following phrases represent the division symbol?
    a. More than
    b. Product of
    c. Quotient of
    d. Results in
    e. Less than

12. Marietta needs a new hat to go with her witch costume for Halloween. She needs to describe what she wants to her mother so her mom can make her hat. Marietta cannot remember the name for the shape of the hat she wants. She knows it's round at the bottom and then rises up to a point at the top. What shape does she want?
    a. Sphere
    b. Diamond
    c. Triangle
    d. Circle
    e. Cone

13. Which two measurements of a triangle are needed to calculate the area of a triangle?
    a. Length, width
    b. Base, height
    c. Perimeter, height
    d. Base, width
    e. Perimeter, base

14. Ava is helping her dad plan out a garden space in their rectangle-shaped backyard. They measured the whole backyard, which was 50 feet long and 37 feet wide. Her dad decided to designate a rectangular back section of the yard, and they plotted out a space that was 20 feet long and 15 feet wide. What is the area of the new garden space?
    a. 1850 square feet
    b. 87 square feet
    c. 300 square feet
    d. 35 square feet
    e. 150 square feet

15. What is an angle measuring less than 90 degrees called?
    a. Obtuse
    b. Right
    c. Complementary
    d. Acute
    e. Straight

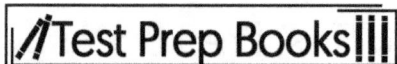

16. Which of the following units would be most appropriate to measure the size of a book?
    a. Millimeters
    b. Feet
    c. Yards
    d. Meters
    e. Inches

17. A basketball team's bake sale was a huge success. The team managed to raise $465. The coach said that after everyone gets a new uniform, the remaining money can be used to buy new basketballs. New uniforms cost $25 each, and there are 13 players on the team. New basketballs cost $10 each. How many basketballs will the team be able to buy?
    a. 46
    b. 5
    c. 14
    d. 140
    e. 13

18. Paul's family is taking a trip next summer. They are going to visit several national parks around the country. His dad says they will drive approximately 1800 miles during their month-long vacation. Paul's dad also said they will need a lot of gas for the car. If the family's car gets approximately 24 miles per gallon, which equation calculates how many gallons of gas they will use throughout the trip?
    a. $1800 \div 24$
    b. $1800 + 24$
    c. $1800 - 24$
    d. 1800×24
    e. $1800(24)$

19. The animal shelter is trying to estimate how many new toys they need to buy next year. They want to round the number of dogs and cats to the nearest ten and get three toys for each animal. If they have 48 dogs and 27 cats, approximately how many toys will they need?
    a. 225
    b. 210
    c. 240
    d. 180
    e. 150

20. Jacinda is going to her first professional car racing event. She is very excited! Her mom told her that there will be 43 cars racing and that they will each go around the track 288 times! How many total combined laps will the cars race by the end of the event?
    a. 288
    b. 12,000
    c. 11,520
    d. 12,900
    e. 12,384

21. The party supply store is having a sale on balloons. They have 25 red ones, 38 blue ones, 19 green ones, 29 yellow ones, and 34 purple ones. What percentage of the balloons are yellow?
   a. 0.20%
   b. 5%
   c. 17%
   d. 20%
   e. 14.5%

22. Mrs. Hansen's class is celebrating Rainbow Day. Each student got to dress up in any color of the rainbow they wanted. There are 34 students in the class. Of those students, 10 wore blue, 12 wore red, 8 wore green, and 4 wore yellow. What fraction represents the number of students who wore red?
   a. $\frac{5}{17}$
   b. $\frac{6}{17}$
   c. $\frac{8}{34}$
   d. $\frac{4}{34}$
   e. $\frac{11}{17}$

23. Isabella just started a new job as a delivery driver. She wants to determine how many miles she drives each day on her route. Look at the figure of Isabella's route and calculate how many miles she drives if she starts and ends at the same point.

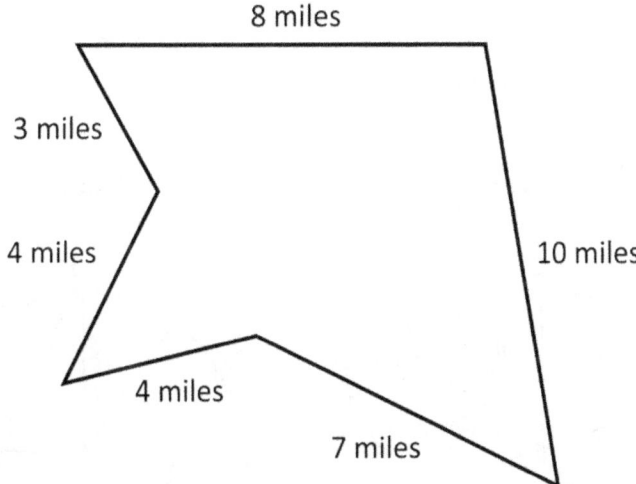

   a. 32
   b. 33
   c. 72
   d. 36
   e. 29

24. Micah needs to figure out exactly how many feet of pipe he needs to finish working on the drain system for his yard. He knows he still needs 150 inches to finish the job, but the pipe is only sold by the foot. How many feet of pipe does he need to buy?
- a. 18
- b. 12.5
- c. 13
- d. 150
- e. 12

25. Henry's house is 3 kilometers from Mia's house. How far is that distance is meters?
- a. 30,000
- b. 30
- c. 300
- d. 0.3
- e. 3,000

26. Anthony, Emily, Christopher, and Ryan went to pick apples. Together they picked a total of 300 apples. Anthony and Emily both picked 75 apples each, Christopher picked 120 apples, and Ryan picked 30 apples. Which circle graph shows the percentage of the total apples that each person picked?

A
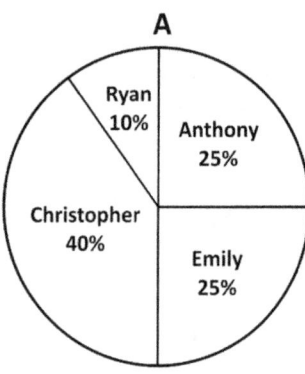

B
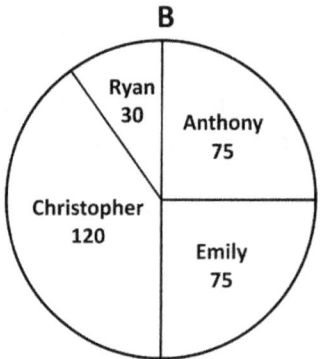

C
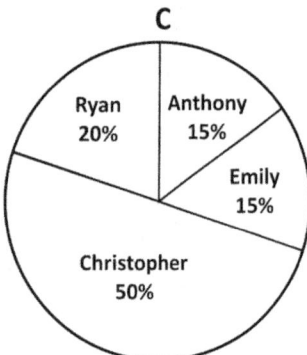

D
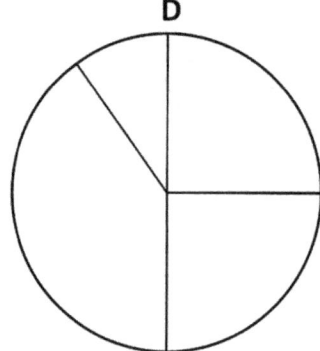

- a. Graph A
- b. Graph B
- c. Graph C
- d. Graph D
- e. None of the graphs correctly show the data.

27. The city of Fairbanks, Alaska, has one of the most extreme temperature ranges in the United States.

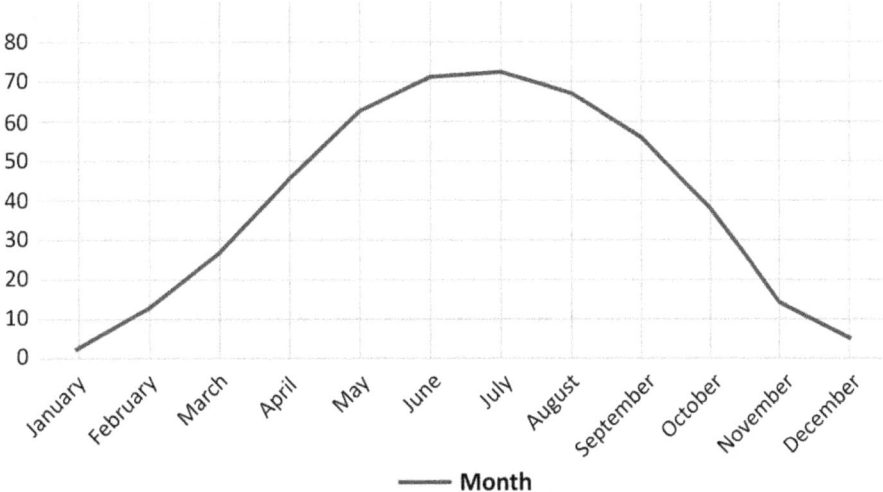

According to the graph, which month has the lowest average temperature?
   a. January
   b. December
   c. June
   d. July
   e. November

28. Brianna drives the library's very popular Bookmobile. She goes to MLK Elementary School on Mondays and Wednesdays and ABC-XYZ Day Camp on Mondays, Wednesdays, and Fridays. She goes to the middle school every Thursday, and the high school has her come by every Tuesday and Friday. She also makes weekly stops at Cute Kids Daycare, Sunrise Elementary, and Forest Middle School and twice weekly stops at Riverside High School and Elm Park Boys and Girls Club. How many stops does Brianna make each week?
   a. 9
   b. 8
   c. 17
   d. 15
   e. 7

29. Claire, Kenneth, Nora, and Max are playing with their race cars and race car track. Claire has 44 inches of track, Kenneth has 26 inches, Nora has 97 inches, and Max has 107 inches. If they put all their tracks together, how long with their racetrack be?
   a. 274 inches
   b. 179 inches
   c. 300 inches
   d. 167 inches
   e. 214 inches

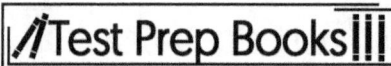

30. Jose and his four friends are comparing the grades they got on the last science test. Jose got $\frac{90}{100}$, Timothy got 0.625, Andrew got 0.87, Mary Jane got $\frac{42}{50}$, and Arya got $\frac{24}{25}$. Who got the highest grade on the test?
    a. Timothy
    b. Jose
    c. Andrew
    d. Mary Jane
    e. Arya

Verbal Section

Synonyms

Each of the questions below has one word, followed by five other words. Please select one answer whose meaning is closest to the word in capital letters.

1. RESEARCH
    a. Criticize
    b. Change
    c. Teach
    d. Investigate
    e. Science

2. LUXURIOUS
    a. Faded
    b. Bright
    c. Fancy
    d. Inconsiderate
    e. Ordinary

3. ABANDON
    a. Find
    b. Replace
    c. Leave
    d. Destroy
    e. Swap

4. OPPRESSED
    a. Acclaimed
    b. Liberated
    c. Beloved
    d. Pressured
    e. Helpless

5. TRIUMPH
    a. Victory
    b. Burial
    c. Animosity
    d. Banter
    e. Emphasis

6. BLAND
    a. Complex
    b. Dull
    c. Novel
    d. Superior
    e. Spicy

7. SPECTATOR
    a. Assistant
    b. Guardian
    c. Observer
    d. Participant
    e. Runner

8. PAMPHLET
    a. Brochure
    b. Letter
    c. Newspaper
    d. Tome
    e. Novel

9. ENCHANT
    a. Complicate
    b. Inform
    c. Construct
    d. Suffice
    e. Mesmerize

10. APPROXIMATE
    a. Define
    b. Estimate
    c. Populate
    d. Subject
    e. Remember

11. JUBILATION
    a. Happiness
    b. Memorial
    c. Pollution
    d. Transformation
    e. Disagreement

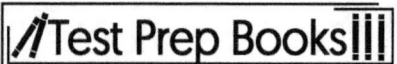

12. THWART
    a. Ignore
    b. Invest
    c. Patronize
    d. Prevent
    e. Assist

13. NONCHALANT
    a. Busy
    b. Intense
    c. Problematic
    d. Unconcerned
    e. Focused

14. TREMOR
    a. Ache
    b. Chill
    c. Shake
    d. Sickness
    e. Fever

15. PROTRUDE
    a. Bulge
    b. Dissect
    c. Insert
    d. Suspect
    e. Begin

Analogies

The questions below ask you to find relationships between words. For each question, select the answer that best completes the meaning of the sentence.

16. Books are to reading as:
    a. Movies are to making
    b. Shows are to watching
    c. Poetry is to writing
    d. Scenes are to performing
    e. Concerts are to music

17. Cool is to frigid as warm is to:
    a. Toasty
    b. Summer
    c. Sweltering
    d. Hot
    e. Mild

18. Cereal boxes are to rectangular prisms as globes are to:
    a. Circles
    b. Maps
    c. Wheels
    d. Spheres
    e. Movement

19. Storm is to rainbow as sunset is to:
    a. Clouds
    b. Sunrise
    c. Breakfast
    d. Bedtime
    e. Stars

20. Mechanic is to repair as:
    a. Mongoose is to cobra
    b. Rider is to bicycle
    c. Tree is to grow
    d. Food is to eaten
    e. Doctor is to heal

21. Whistle is to trumpet as painting is to:
    a. View
    b. Criticize
    c. Sculpture
    d. Painter
    e. Paintbrush

22. Winter is to autumn as summer is to:
    a. Vacation
    b. Spring
    c. Fall
    d. March
    e. Weather

23. Wool is to sweater as:
    a. Bamboo is to panda
    b. Capital is to D.C.
    c. Copper is to penny
    d. Flint is to sharpening
    e. Wind is to windmill

24. Rose is to flower as:
    a. Daisy is to pollen
    b. Cat is to catnip
    c. Surgeon is to doctor
    d. Radiology is to disease
    e. Nutrition is to reproduction

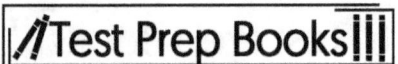

25. Whisk is to baking as:
    a. Glove is to boxing
    b. Swimming is to water
    c. Love is to romance
    d. Azalea is to flower
    e. Bench is to park

26. Old age is to youth as:
    a. Transparent is to opaque
    b. Soldier is to war
    c. Subtle is to sophisticated
    d. Yellow is to happiness
    e. Surly is to scandalous

27. Lying is to distrust as:
    a. Prohibit is to outlaw
    b. Petulant is to children
    c. Exploit is to gain
    d. Imprudent is to money
    e. Hurricane is to devastation

28. Desolate is to barren as:
    a. Defend is to prosecute
    b. Preserve is to maintain
    c. Avid is to cheerleader
    d. Bittersweet is to happiness
    e. King is to ambition

29. Carpenter is to construction as:
    a. Adaptation is to insect
    b. Acquisition is to possession
    c. Wizard is to magic
    d. Baker is to bread
    e. Microsoft is to programming

30. Car is to transport as:
    a. Radio is to sound
    b. Volume is to voice
    c. Triangles are to circles
    d. Fireplace is to heat
    e. Mangos are to fruit

Reading Section

Read the following passage, and then answer questions 1-5.

A lot of people believe that 75% of your body heat is lost through your head. I had certainly heard this before, and I'm not going to attempt to say I didn't believe it when I first heard it. It is natural to be gullible to anything said strongly enough. But the "fact" that the majority of your body heat is lost through your head is a lie.

Let me explain. Heat loss is based on the amount of "surface area" of skin that is exposed. An elephant loses a lot more heat than an anteater because it has a much greater surface area than an anteater. Each cell in the body produces energy in the form of heat. It takes a lot more energy to run an elephant than an anteater. So, each part of your body loses an amount of heat based on the size of its skin. The human torso probably loses the most heat, though the legs lose a significant amount as well. Some people have asked, "Why does it feel so much warmer when you cover your head than when you don't?" Well, that's because your head loses a lot of heat when it is not clothed, while the clothing on the rest of your body provides insulation. If you went outside with a hat and pants but no shirt, not only would you look silly, but your heat loss would be a lot greater because so much more of you would be exposed. So, if given the choice to cover your chest or your head in the cold, choose the chest.

1. Why does the author compare elephants and anteaters?
    a. To express an opinion
    b. To give an example that helps clarify the main point
    c. To show the differences between the two
    d. To persuade why one is better than the other
    e. To educate about animals

2. Which of the following best describes the tone of the passage?
    a. Harsh
    b. Angry
    c. Casual
    d. Indifferent
    e. Comical

3. What does the word *gullible* mean in paragraph 1?
    a. To be angry toward
    b. To distrust something
    c. To believe something easily
    d. To be happy toward
    e. To be frightened

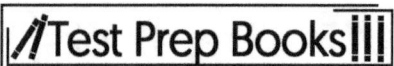

4. What is the main idea of the passage?
    a. To illustrate how people can easily believe anything they are told
    b. To prove that you have to have a hat to survive in the cold
    c. To persuade the audience that anteaters are better than elephants
    d. To convince the audience that heat loss comes mostly from the head
    e. To debunk the myth that heat loss comes mostly from the head

5. Based on the passage, which article of clothing would provide the LEAST insulation?
    a. Coat
    b. Pants
    c. Shirt
    d. Gloves
    e. Jacket

Read the following passage, and answer the question below.

> Samuel teaches at a high school in one of the biggest cities in the United States. His students come from diverse family backgrounds. Samuel observes that the best students in his class are from homes where parents are most involved. The bottom five students are from homes where parental supervision is minimal, by a large margin. There are 24 students in his class.

6. What is true about the students that Samuel teaches?
    a. They are not a diverse group of students.
    b. The students with the most involved parents have the best academic performance.
    c. The worst students in his class have the most parental supervision.
    d. Only five students have parents that are heavily involved.
    e. A larger class size would increase student performance.

Read the following passage, and answer the question below.

> A famous children's author recently published a historical fiction novel under a fake name; however, it did not sell as many copies as her children's books. In her earlier years, she had majored in history and earned a graduate degree in Antebellum American History, which is the when her new novel happens. Critics praised this newest book far more than the children's series that made her famous. In fact, her new novel was nominated for the prestigious Albert J. Beveridge Award but still isn't selling like her children's books, which sell a lot of copies because of her name alone.

7. What made the children's author famous?
    a. Being nominated for a prestigious award
    b. Her historical fiction novel
    c. Her children's series
    d. Using a fake name for her new novel
    e. Earning a graduate degree

Read the following passage, and answer the question below.

> Reggie had been preparing for his part in the play for several months. His mother had even knitted him a costume. That night when he went on stage, his entire family and all his friends were there to watch, and he was mortified when his costume split in half. Afterwards, his mother admitted that she was not the best at knitting.

8. When did Reggie's costume split in half?
    a. While he was preparing for the play
    b. While his mother was knitting it
    c. During the play
    d. After the play
    e. His costume did not split in half

Read the following passage, and answer the question below.

> The reason for different breeds of dogs is that there were specific needs that humans wanted to fill with their animals. For example, scent hounds are known for their extraordinary ability to track game through smelling their scent. These breeds are also known for their endurance in seeking deer and other prey. Therefore, early hunters took dogs that displayed these abilities and bred them to encourage these traits.

9. What is the main purpose of the passage?
    a. To explain the abilities and traits of scent hounds
    b. To describe early hunting techniques
    c. To promote dog ownership for pets
    d. To show that scent hounds are the best breed for hunting
    e. To explain one of the needs of humans that was filled by breeding dogs

Read the following passage, and then answer questions 10-11.

> The big RV, or Recreational Vehicle, was a great purchase for our family and brought us all closer together. Every morning we would wake up, eat breakfast, and pack up our things. We laughed at our own comical attempts to back "The Beast" into spaces that seemed impossibly small. When things inevitably went wrong and we couldn't solve the problems on our own, we discovered the incredible helpfulness and friendliness of the RV community. We even made some new friends in the process.

10. According the passage, what did the family discover?
    a. The best way to back an RV into small spaces
    b. That the RV community is friendly and helpful
    c. That as a family they could solve problems on their own without any help
    d. That it's impossible to make friends when you break camp each morning
    e. That it isn't funny when you experience problems

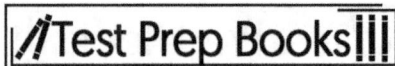

11. What is the most likely reason that the family calls their RV "The Beast"?
    a. The vehicle was scary to look at.
    b. The family didn't like riding in the RV because it was uncomfortable.
    c. The RV was too expensive and it was not worth the price.
    d. Driving in the RV made the family have serious disagreements.
    e. The RV was very large and could be difficult to control.

Read the following passage, and answer the question below.

> Koko the gorilla, who passed in 2018 at the age of forty-six, knew more than 2,000 words and could sign at least 1,000 of those. Although this was impressive by itself, even more interesting was the belief that Koko, in addition to learning words, was actually communicating with the researchers she worked with. Perhaps even more interesting, in terms of language learning, is that Koko created her own word combinations for words she didn't know. For example, she coined "eye hats" to mean a mask and, more famously, "finger watches" to mean rings.

12. Why was Koko's communication most interesting?
    a. She had a vocabulary of 2,000 words.
    b. She created new words.
    c. She could sign 1,000 words.
    d. She had the ability to acquire vocabulary.
    e. She lived to 46 years old.

Read the following passage, and then answer questions 13-14.

> Raul is going to Egypt next month. He has been looking forward to this vacation all year. Since childhood, Raul has been fascinated with pyramids, especially the Great Pyramid of Giza, which is the oldest of the Seven Wonders of the Ancient World. According to religious custom, Egyptian royalty is buried in the tombs located within the pyramid's great labyrinths. Since it has been many years since Raul read about the pyramid's history, he wants to read a book describing how and why the Egyptians built the Great Pyramid thousands of years ago.

13. How long has Raul been excited about his vacation to Egypt?
    a. Since childhood
    b. All month
    c. All year
    d. Many years
    e. A few days

14. How do we know that the Great Pyramid of Giza is very old?
    a. It was the tomb for many people.
    b. There have been books written about the Great Pyramid of Giza.
    c. Royalty was buried in the pyramid's great labyrinths.
    d. The Great Pyramid of Giza is located in Egypt.
    e. It is one of the Seven Wonders of the Ancient World.

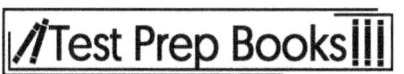

Read the following passage, and answer the question below.

> After many failed attempts, Julio made a solemn promise to his mother to clean his room. When she came home from a long day of work, she found her son playing video games, and his room still a disaster. Her fists clenched, her eyebrows lowered, and she stared down her son and delivered an angry speech that made him hang his head regretfully.

15. What did Julio break?
    a. His video game
    b. Nothing
    c. Everything in his room
    d. His promise
    e. His mother's work

Read the following passage, and then answer questions 16-19.

> Moths and butterflies both have a life cycle that includes a caterpillar stage before they take their final form, and both go through a phase of metamorphosis during which they make the changes to their bodies that they need to grow wings and take flight. Moths wrap themselves in silky shells called cocoons to cover themselves while these changes take place, while butterflies create a hard exoskeleton around themselves called a chrysalis. Without this protection, moths and butterflies could not survive their transformation, so these coverings should not be disturbed.

16. Which of the following do butterflies and moths NOT have in common?
    a. They both go through a phase where they transform their bodies.
    b. They both have wings and can fly when they reach their final form.
    c. They both transform their bodies inside a cocoon.
    d. They both were caterpillars to start with and have to change into their final form.
    e. They both need some kind of covering during their metamorphosis.

17. Which of these things would probably be okay to do with a cocoon or chrysalis?
    a. Cut it open
    b. Microwave it
    c. Hit it
    d. Play with it
    e. Look at it

18. What does the word *metamorphosis* mean in the passage?
    a. A change of form
    b. A change of location
    c. A way to fly
    d. A kind of insect
    e. A kind of caterpillar

113

19. Which of the following things does the passage explain?
    a. All of the steps of the change that happens inside a cocoon or chrysalis
    b. What kind of leaves butterfly and moth caterpillars each eat
    c. How to encourage a butterfly or moth caterpillar to change
    d. That butterflies and moths need their covering to survive the change
    e. Who first discovered the metamorphosis of butterflies and moths

Read the following passage, and then answer questions 20-22.

"Somebody has to stop him!" Sally cried. "He's going to fall!"

Jordan thought Sally was being a little silly. He had climbed higher than this before, and he just needed to go up a tiny bit farther to get his ball. "I am *not* going to fall," he called down to the kids who were gathered around the big tree.

Akash wasn't sure he believed this, but he was afraid to fall himself if he climbed up after Jordan to stop him. He whispered to Sally that she should go get her mom, and then he stared up helplessly as his friend continued his climb.

20. What does "Sally cried" mean in the following sentence?

    "Somebody has to stop him!" Sally cried. "He's going to fall!"

    a. Sally was crying because she was so worried about Jordan.
    b. Sally was shouting about Jordan being up in the tree.
    c. Sally was very calm and not worried about Jordan at all.
    d. Sally was angry with Jordan and was yelling at him.
    e. Sally was determined to climb up that tree herself.

21. Which of these is something that Akash believes will happen?
    a. He will fall if he tries to climb up and stop Jordan.
    b. Jordan will succeed at climbing without falling.
    c. Sally will fail to get her mother in time to help Jordan.
    d. Jordan will hit him if he tries to stop him right now.
    e. Somebody else will fix this problem without them needing to do anything.

22. What might be good advice to give Akash in this story?
    a. Don't climb trees without supervision. You could get hurt.
    b. Don't encourage Sally. She is being mean to your friend Jordan.
    c. You can try to talk Jordan out of this instead of climbing up after him.
    d. You can choose new friends to hang out with rather than staying here.
    e. Your mom would probably do a better job helping than Sally's mom.

Read the following passage, and then answer questions 23-25.

Spring is a great time for flowers. After the ice and snow of winter start to melt, plants that were unable to handle the harshness of such cold conditions are able to grow and thrive again. The flowers have the instructions for how to bloom built right into their genes. Would you believe that the process is started by only a single protein in the flowers' cells? It's true! As the daylight hours increase, a protein called *CONSTANS* is activated inside the plant, and then the flowering can begin.

23. What allows flowers to bloom again when spring begins?
    a. A protein activated by an increase in daylight hours
    b. The ice and snow of winter that are still on the ground
    c. The instructions that people give them for blooming
    d. The process of making proteins in their bodies
    e. The harshness of cold conditions

24. What do we NOT know about *CONSTANS* from the passage?
    a. It is a protein.
    b. It exists inside flowering plants.
    c. It is activated by an increase in daylight hours during the spring.
    d. It has this name for helping flowers bloom at a "constant" time.
    e. It is what begins the process of flowers blooming in spring.

25. Which of these sentences from the passage states an opinion rather than sharing a fact or facts?
    a. "After the ice and snow of winter start to melt, plants that were unable to handle the harshness of such cold conditions are able to grow and thrive again."
    b. "As the daylight hours increase, a protein called *CONSTANS* is activated inside the plant, and then the flowering can begin."
    c. "The flowers have the instructions for how to bloom built right into their genes."
    d. "Spring is a great time for flowers."
    e. "It's true!"

Read the following passage, and then answer questions 26-28.

The tiger's tail whipped impatiently behind him as he once again prepared to pounce. He would get his human prey this time! Wait for it... wait for it... GO!

Just as the tiger had all of his muscles tensed to dive for his prey, the bigger one returned yet *again* to complicate matters. The little human boy was no match for the tiger all alone and would make a lovely midmorning snack. The bigger human was also no match for the tiger, he told himself, but it would take far too much effort to deal with him. It wasn't worth the effort.

The tiger slunk off in annoyance, abandoning his potential snack. Humans didn't taste very good anyway, he thought to himself.

26. Why was the tiger impatient at the start of the passage?
    a. He had to leave without eating his snack.
    b. He had gone hungry for days before this.
    c. He was annoyed that humans didn't taste very good.
    d. He kept being interrupted while stalking his prey.
    e. He wanted a human friend and couldn't have one.

27. Why did seeing "the bigger one" cause the tiger to hold back and eventually leave?
    a. That one looked like he could put up a real fight that the tiger couldn't win.
    b. Dealing with that one would be too much work just for a quick snack.
    c. The tiger wasn't hungry enough to eat that one, too.
    d. The bigger one could see him, and he couldn't have that.
    e. The big ones were slow, which would take the fun out of the hunt.

28. Which of these statements is most likely to be true about the tiger?
    a. He is the only tiger in the jungle, so the villagers assume they are safe.
    b. He has humans for snacks every day.
    c. He lives close enough to humans to consider having this boy for a quick snack.
    d. He usually only eats deer.
    e. His favorite food is little human boys, so this was a big disappointment for him.

Writing Sample

Tell a story using the picture below. Make sure that your story has a beginning, middle, and end.

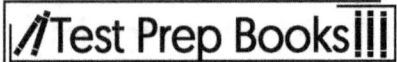

The following pages are provided for writing your story.

Answer Explanations

Quantitative Section

1. B: 80 is a multiple of 8 because it is equal to 8 times 10. 32 is a multiple of 8 because it is equal to 8 times 4. 48 is a multiple of 8 because it is equal to 8 times 6. 16 is a multiple of 8 because it is equal to 8 times 2. 2 is not a multiple of 8. It is actually a factor of 8.

2. E: To find the value of the sum, line up the numbers and then add each column individually working from right to left. $3 + 2 = 5$. $3 + 9 = 12$. Therefore, carry the 1 to the next column and leave the 2 in that place value. $1 + 2 + 5 = 8$. Putting these values together, the answer is 825.

3. B: Order of operations must be followed. First, perform the multiplication and division from left to right. This leaves the expression $2 + 24 - 2$. Then, perform the addition and subtraction from left to right. The answer is 24.

4. E: The answer can easily be seen by changing each fraction to its corresponding decimal form. $\frac{1}{4}$ is equivalent to 0.25, $\frac{2}{3}$ is equivalent to $0.\overline{6}$, $\frac{6}{7}$ is around 0.857, $\frac{1}{2}$ is equivalent to 0.5, and $\frac{3}{8}$ is equivalent to 0.375. The fractions given in the problem are $\frac{1}{3} = 0.\overline{3}$ and $\frac{2}{5} = 0.4$. Therefore, the correct answer is $\frac{3}{8} = 0.375$.

5. A: To add decimals, place the decimals on top of each other making sure to line up the decimal points. Then, add column by column starting from the right. 2.3 is equivalent to 2.30. Therefore, 5.67 + 2.3 = 7.97.

6. E: Morgan will need to do 22 more minutes of exercise to reach his goal of 3 hours for the week. The information given in hours must be converted to minutes, and then the following equation can be used to find the solution.

$$\left(3 \text{ hours} \times \frac{60 \text{ minutes}}{1 \text{ hour}}\right) - 35 \text{ minutes} - 22 \text{ minutes} - 41 \text{ minutes} - \left(1 \text{ hour} \times \frac{60 \text{ minutes}}{1 \text{ hour}}\right)$$

7. E: In this bar graph, 5 children prefer brownies and cake. The children columns for brownies and cake have heights of 3 and 2, respectively. Added together that makes a total of 5 children.

8. D: The expanded or decomposed form represents the sum of each place value of a number. The numbers are added back together to find the standard form of the number.

9. C: The method used to convert a fraction to a decimal is to divide the numerator by the denominator.

10. D: Three girls for every two boys can be expressed as a ratio: $3:2$. This can be visualized as splitting the school into five groups: three girl groups and two boy groups. The number of students that are in each group can be found by dividing the total number of students by five:

$$\frac{650 \text{ students}}{5 \text{ groups}} = \frac{130 \text{ students}}{\text{group}}$$

Answer Explanations

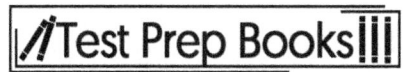

To find the total number of girls, multiply the number of students per group (130) by the number of girl groups in the school (3). This equals 390, Choice *D*.

11. C: Phrases such as *divided by*, *quotient of*, or *half of* can all be used to indicate the use of the division symbol in a mathematical expression. *More than* typically indicates the addition symbol. The multiplication symbol is represented by the phrase *product of*. *Results in* is another way to say equal to and is shown by the equal sign. *Less than* is often used for subtraction and uses the minus sign.

12. E: Marietta wants a hat shaped like a cone. A cone is a 3-dimensional figure that looks like a circle with a triangle on top of it. A sphere, Choice *A*, is a shape such as a ball. Choices *B*, *C* and *D* are two-dimensional, flat shapes.

13. B: The correct formula for calculating the area of a triangle is $A = \frac{1}{2} \times b \times h$, where A is equal to area, b is equal to base, and h is equal to height. Therefore, the two measurements needed to calculate the area of a triangle are base and height.

14. C: Area is measured by multiplying the length times the width: $20 \times 15 = 300$ sq. ft. Choice *A* is the area for the whole backyard rather than just the area of the garden space, and Choice *B* adds the measurements for the whole backyard instead of multiplying. Choice *D* uses the correct measurements but adds them instead of multiplying them. Choice *E* divides the measurements in half, similar to finding the area of a triangle by taking half of the base times width.

15. D: An angle measuring less than 90 degrees is called an acute angle. An angle measuring more than 90 degrees is an obtuse angle. A right angle is an angle that measures 90 degrees. A complementary angle is one of two angles which when added together equal 90 degrees. A straight angle is 180 degrees.

16. E: The most appropriate unit to use when measuring the size of a book is inches. This is based on the knowledge of the approximate size of most books and knowing the approximate size of the unit of measurement. Meters, yards, and feet are too large for most books, while millimeters are too small.

17. C: The team will spend $325 on the new uniforms ($25 times 13 players). There will be $140 left over. The basketballs cost $10 each. $140 divided by $10 means that the team can get 14 new basketballs. Choice *A* forgot to buy the uniforms first and instead spent all the money on basketballs. Choice *B* counts the same price of $25 for the basketballs and the uniforms. Choice *D* is the amount of money left over rather than the number of basketballs the team can buy. Choice *E* is the number of players on the team, not the number of basketballs that the team can buy.

18. A: The way to solve this problem is to divide the number of miles the family will drive by the number of miles per gallon that the car can travel: $1800 \div 24 = 75$. So, the car will go through 75 gallons of gas during the trip. Choices *B*, *C*, *D*, and *E* use incorrect operations (adding, subtracting, and multiplying).

19. C: Both the number of dogs and the number of cats need to be rounded up, meaning that they have 50 dogs and 30 cats. Adding those together equals 80 animals. Then, multiply the number of animals times 3 toys for each, which means they will need approximately 240 toys. Choice *A* is the exact total rather than an estimation. Choice *B* rounds the number of dogs up to 50 but rounds the number of cats down to 20 rather than up to 30. Choice *D* rounds the numbers of dogs and cats down rather than up. Choice *E* includes the rounded figure of 50 dogs, but it fails to add the rounded number of 30 cats before multiplying by three.

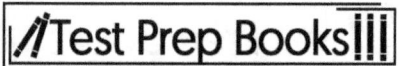

Answer Explanations

20. E: To solve this problem, multiply the number of cars times the number of laps they will each run: $43 \times 288 = 12{,}384$ laps. Choice A is just the total laps; it does not count that each car will race all those laps. Choice B uses rounding to estimate the total rather than calculating the exact number of laps raced. Similarly, Choice C rounds the number of cars and multiplies that by the number of laps. Choice D rounds the number of times around the track to 300.

21. D: The first step is to find out how many balloons the store has in total: $25 + 38 + 19 + 29 + 34 = 145$. Then, divide the number of yellow balloons by the total number of balloons: $29 \div 145 = 0.20$. Move the decimal two places to the right to get the percentage. Choice A forgot to move the decimal. Choice B divided the number of total balloons by the number of yellow balloons instead of the other way around, and Choice C calculated the percentage of red balloons rather than the yellow ones. Choice D just divides the total number of balloons by ten.

22. B: The number of students who wore red was 12 out of 34 students, which creates the fraction $\frac{12}{34}$. That can be reduced to $\frac{6}{17}$ students. Choice A is the number of students who wore blue, Choice B is the unreduced fraction of students who wore green, and Choice D is the unreduced fraction of students who wore yellow. Choice E is the fraction of students who did not wear red.

23. D: To calculate the distance Isabella drives, add the number of miles shown on each section of the route: $8 + 10 + 7 + 4 + 4 + 3 = 36$ mi. Choices A and B both add the number of miles but forget to include the miles back to the starting point (either 3 or 4, depending on the direction around the route). Choice C adds the miles around the route twice. Choice E misses the 7-mile segment.

24. C: There are 12 inches in one foot, so to convert from inches to feet, divide the number of inches by 12. In this case, 150 inches divided by 12 equals 12.5 feet. However, the question notes that pipe is only sold by the foot, so we need to round up to 13 feet, so the answer must be Choice C, 13 feet.

25. E: One kilometer equals 1000 meters, so 3 kilometers equals 3000 meters. Choice A is the distance in decimeters, Choice B is dekameters, and Choice C is hectometers.

26. A: To solve this problem, figure out the percentage for each person by dividing the number of apples they picked by the total number of apples and multiplying by 100. For example, the equation to find Anthony's and Emily's share is $75 \div 300 = 0.25 \times 100 = 25\%$. Anthony and Emily each picked 25%, or $\frac{1}{4}$ of the total. Christopher picked 40%, and Ryan picked 10%. Choose the pie graph that reflects those percentages. Choice B shows the correct graph, but it is labeled by number rather than by percentages. Choice C shows incorrect percentages, even though it does show Christopher as picking the most apples, and Choice D is missing all the labels.

27. A: The lowest temperature in Fairbanks, 2 degrees, occurs in January. Choice B, December, is close but is the second lowest. Choices C and D show the two warmest months. Choice E, November, shows a month with a sharp drop from the previous month, but it is not the lowest average temperature.

28. D: To solve this problem, add all of Brianna's current stops each week: 2 for MLK; 3 for ABC; 1 for the middle school; 2 for the high school; 1 each for Cute Kids, Sunrise, and Forest Middle; and 2 each for Riverside and Elm Park. $2 + 3 + 1 + 2 + 1 + 1 + 1 + 2 + 2 = 15$ stops each week. Choice A counted the number of places but did not include places that have multiple stops. Choice B only counted the specific days that are listed but did not include the places with weekly stops where no specific day was

Answer Explanations

noted. Choice *C* counted all of the stops but incorrectly added two more. Choice *E* fails to count stops at there of the locations.

29. A: The way to solve this problem is to add each of the four numbers together. Choice *B* adds the numbers incorrectly, Choice *C* adds the numbers correctly but includes Kenneth's track twice, and Choice *D* does not include Max's track.

30. E: When all the grades are converted to percentages, Jose scored 90%, Timothy got 62.5%, Andrew earned 87%, Mary Jane scored 84%, and Arya's grade was 96%. So, Arya, the student with $\frac{24}{25}$, or 96%, got the highest score. Choices *B*, *C*, and *D* are the next three highest scores in order, with Choice *A*, Timothy, having the lowest score.

Verbal Section

Synonyms

1. D: Research is closest in meaning to *investigate*. When someone does research, they look things up in different resources like books and journals, or they may conduct a scientific study, which is also called an investigation.

2. C: *Fancy* is the best synonym for *luxurious*—both describe elaborate and/or elegant lifestyles and/or settings.

3. C: To abandon something is most like leaving it. Finding or replacing something is unrelated to abandoning it and *destroy* is a more active and destructive word than *abandon*.

4. E: The word *oppressed* means being exploited or helpless, Choice *E*. Choice *A*, *acclaimed*, means being praised. To be *liberated* is to be free. To be beloved, Choice *C*, means to be cherished and adored. To be pressured, Choice *D*, means to be pushed into doing something, in some contexts.

5. A: The word *triumph* most closely means victory, Choice *A*. *Burial*, Choice *B*, is the act of burying someone or something. *Animosity*, Choice *C*, means strong dislike or hatred, and is very different from the word *triumph*. Choice *D*, *banter*, is the act of teasing. Choice *E*, *emphasis*, is to give something special importance.

6. B: *Bland* is an adjective that can mean lacking in strong, defining characteristics, and, as a result, uninteresting. *Complex*, *novel*, and *superior* are all adjectives that themselves refer to strong or defining characteristics—by describing something as *complex*, *novel*, or *superior*, one is describing something as being, in one way or another, interesting. *Dull*, on the other hand, is an adjective that can be defined as lacking interest or excitement, and it is therefore synonymous with the word *bland*. In terms of taste, a *spicy* food is an opposite of *bland*.

7. C: *Spectator* is a noun that means a person who looks on, or watches. *Assistant*, *guardian*, *participant*, and *runner* are all nouns describing people involved in a certain process or action—the act of assisting, guarding, participating, or running—rather than someone who is just watching something occur. *Observer* is a noun meaning an individual who observes, and the verb phrases *watches* or *looks on* and *observes* are synonyms. Therefore, *observer* is a synonymous term with *spectator*.

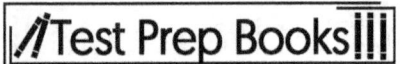

Answer Explanations

8. A: *Pamphlet* is a noun that refers to any small booklet that contains information or arguments about a single subject. The noun *letter* can refer to any written communication, but a letter generally refers to a private communication, whereas a *pamphlet* is usually used to spread information publicly. While a *newspaper* and a *pamphlet* both represent public means of written communication, a *pamphlet* is generally smaller than a newspaper, and is usually more focused on a single topic. A *tome*, which is a noun referring to a large, scholarly book, is much more massive in physical size and scope than a *pamphlet*. A *novel* is a long chapter book. A *brochure*, which is a noun defined as a small book containing information about a product or service, is functionally the same as a *pamphlet*, and the two words are synonymous.

9. E: *Enchant* is a verb that can be defined as either to subject to magical influence or to fill one with delight. The verb *complicate*, which can be defined as to make difficult, has no connection to the idea of magic and is clearly unrelated to the concept of delight. *Inform* is a verb that simply means to give or impart knowledge and *suffice* is a verb that simply means to be adequate or enough. *Construct* means to build something. Therefore, none of these are related to the ideas of delight or magical influence. *Mesmerize* is a verb that means either to hypnotize or to fascinate, and therefore is closely synonymous with *enchant*.

10. B: *Approximate,* as a verb, means to come near to or nearly meet. *Define* is a verb that means to determine the meaning or boundary of, so it's more specific than an approximation. *Populate* means to settle in or fill an area, which has nothing to do with the word *approximate*. *Subject,* as a verb, means to control someone or something, or to expose them to certain conditions. To *remember* is to draw something from your memory. *Estimate* means to approximately calculate and it's directly synonymous with *approximate*.

11. A: *Jubilation* is a noun meaning a feeling of or expression of joy. Accordingly, *happiness* is a directly synonymous term. *Memorial, pollution, transformation,* and *disagreement* are all nouns that express concepts that are not necessarily—or at all—related to the concept of joy or happiness.

12. D: *Thwart* is a verb meaning to oppose successfully and prevent from fulfilling an intended purpose. *Invest* is a verb that means to support a cause, which is nearly the opposite meaning of *thwart*. *Patronize* means to talk down to someone and has nothing to do with thwart. *Ignore* is defined as to refrain from noticing, so it is not similar to *thwart,* either. *Assist* is an opposite of *thwart*, as it means to help with something. *Prevent*, a verb meaning to keep from happening, is synonymous with *thwart*.

13. D: *Nonchalant* is an adjective that can be best defined as coolly unconcerned or indifferent and is therefore directly synonymous with the term *unconcerned*. *Busy, intense, problematic,* and *focused* are all adjectives that describe stress-provoking moods or atmospheres, making them nearly opposite in meaning to *nonchalant*.

14. C: *Tremor* is a noun that can be defined as an involuntary quivering motion. *Shake,* as a noun, refers to the act of trembling or shivering, both of which are synonymous with quivering. *Ache, chill, sickness,* and *fever* are related to the word *tremor* because of the connection to cold air and physical illness, but they are not synonymous terms.

15. A: *Protrude* is a verb that means to project or thrust forward. *Suspect* is a verb that means to believe to be guilty and is not a physical action verb like *protrude.* To *begin* is to start something, which is unrelated to the meaning of *protrude*. *Dissect* and *insert* are both physical action verbs, but have distinct

124

Answer Explanations

meanings, with *dissect* meaning to cut open and *insert* meaning to place in. *Bulge* is a verb meaning to swell or bend outward and is therefore synonymous with the verb *protrude*.

Analogies

16. B: This is a tool/use analogy. The common thread is audience response to an art form. Choices *A*, *C*, and *D* deal with the creation of artwork instead of its consumption. Choice *E* describes a form of art instead of the audience engagement with such.

17. C: This is an intensity analogy. The common thread is degree of severity. While *A*, *D*, and *E* can all describe warmth, they don't convey the harshness of sweltering. *B* simply describes a time when people may be more likely to think of warmth.

18. D: This is a characteristic analogy and is based on matching objects to their geometric shapes. Choice *A* is not correct because globes are three-dimensional, whereas circles exist in two dimensions. While wheels are three-dimensional, they are not always solid or perfectly round.

19. E: This is a sequence of events analogy. The common thread is celestial cause-and-effect. Not everyone has breakfast or goes to bed after sunset. Sunrise is not typically thought of as the next interesting celestial event after sunsets. While clouds can develop after sunsets, they are also present before and during this activity. Stars, however, can be seen after dark.

20. E: This is a provider/provision analogy. This analogy looks at professionals and what their job is. Just as a mechanic's job is to repair machinery, a doctor works to heal patients.

21. C: This is a category analogy. Both whistles and trumpets are devices used to project/produce sound. Therefore, the analogy is based on finding something of a categorical nature. While *A*, *B*, *D*, and *E* involve or describe painting, they do not pertain to a distinct discipline alongside painting. Sculpture, however, is another form of art and expression, just like painting.

22. B: This is a sequence of events analogy. This analogy pairs one season with the season that precedes it. Winter is paired with autumn because autumn comes before winter. Out of all the answers, only *B* and *C* are actual seasons. Fall is another name for autumn, which comes after summer, not before. Spring, of course, is the season that comes before summer, making it the right answer.

23. C: This is a source/comprised of analogy. This analogy focuses on pairing a raw material with an object that it's used to create. Wool is used to knit sweaters, just as copper is used in the creation of pennies. While wind powers a windmill, there is no physical object produced, like with the wool/sweater pair.

24. C: This is a category analogy. Remember that we have to figure out the relationship between the first two words so that we can determine the relationship of the answer. Rose is related to flower by type. Rose is a type of flower, just as surgeon is a type of doctor.

25. A: Usually, a *whisk* is a cooking utensil used in the process of *baking*. As such, a *glove* is used in the sport of *boxing*. Both are objects used within a particular process.

26. A: This is considered an antonym analogy. *Youth* is the opposite of old age. Likewise, *transparent* means to see through something, while *opaque* means cloudy or muddy.

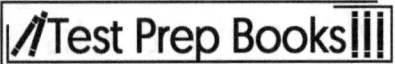

Answer Explanations

27. E: This is a cause and effect analogy. *Lying* causes *distrust,* while *hurricanes* cause *devastation*.

28. B: This is a synonym analogy. *Desolate* and *barren* both mean deserted. Likewise, *preserve* and *maintain* are synonyms.

29. C: This is a performer to related action analogy. We know that *carpenters* perform *construction*, just as *wizards* perform *magic*.

30. D: This is an object/function analogy. The *car* (object) has the function of *transporting* people from one place to the other. Likewise, the function of a *fireplace* is to *heat* up a room.

Reading Section

1. B: Choice *B* is correct because the author is trying to demonstrate the main idea, which is that heat loss is proportional to surface area, so they compare two animals with different surface areas to clarify the main point. Choice *A* is incorrect because the author uses elephants and anteaters to prove a point, that heat loss is based on surface area, not to express an opinion. Choice *C* is incorrect because though the author does use them to show differences, they do so in order to give examples that prove the above points. Choice *D* is incorrect because there is no language to indicate favoritism between the two animals. Choice *E* is incorrect because the passage is not about animals and only uses the elephant and the anteater to make a point.

2. C: Because of the way the author addresses the reader and the casual language the author uses (e.g., "let me explain," "so," "well," "didn't," "you would look silly"), Choice *C* is the best answer because it has a much more casual tone than the usual informative article. Choice *A* may be a tempting choice because the author says the "fact" that most of one's heat is lost through their head is a "lie" and that someone who does not wear a shirt in the cold looks silly. However, this only happens twice within the passage, and the passage does not give an overall tone of harshness. Choice *B* is incorrect because again, while not necessarily nice, the language does not carry an angry charge. The author is clearly not indifferent to the subject because of the passionate language that they use, so Choice *D* is incorrect. Choice *E* is incorrect because the author is not trying to show or use humor in the passage.

3. C: *Gullible* means to believe something easily. The other answer choices could fit easily within the context of the passage: you can be angry toward, distrustful toward, frightened by, or happy toward authority. For this answer choice and the surrounding context, however, the author talks about a myth that people believe easily, so *gullible* would be the word that fits best in this context.

4. E: The whole passage is dedicated to debunking the head heat loss myth. The passage says that "each part of your body loses its proportional amount of heat in accordance with its surface area," which means an area such as the chest would lose more heat than the head because it's bigger. The other answer choices are incorrect.

5. D: The passage focuses only on insulation as it relates to surface area. Since gloves would cover the least surface area of the given options, Choice *D* is correct. A coat, shirt and jacket, Choices *A, C,* and *E,* would cover the torso, while pants, Choice *B,* would cover the legs; the torso and legs each have more surface area than the hands.

6. B: The passage states that the parents of the top five students are the most involved. Choice *A* is incorrect because the passage states that Samuel's students come from diverse backgrounds. Choice *C* is

Answer Explanations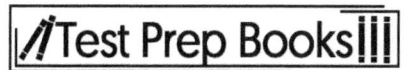

incorrect because Samuel has observed that the worst students have minimal parental supervision, not the most supervision. Choice D is incorrect because the passage does not give the number of students who have involved parents. It only states that the best students have involved parents. Five is the number of the students who have minimal parental supervision. There are 19 other students in the class, but even with this information, we cannot determine how many students have involved parents. Some parents might be right in the middle, providing moderate supervision. The passage does not say anything about larger or smaller class sizes, so Choice E is incorrect.

7. C: It is stated in the passage that her new work was praised far more than the children's series that made her famous. Therefore, Choice C is correct. Choice A is incorrect because while she was nominated for the Albert J. Beveridge Award, this is not what made her famous. Choice B is incorrect because although critics praised her new historical fiction novel more than they praised her children's series, it's the children's series, not the new novel, that made her famous. Choice D is incorrect because the author did not become famous for using a fake name. She was already famous for her children's series before she wrote a new novel under a fake name. Choice E is incorrect because earning an advanced degree did not make her famous.

8. C: The passage states that on the night Reggie went on stage he was mortified when his costume split in half. Choice A is incorrect. His costume did not split in half while he was preparing for the play. Choice B is incorrect. It did not split open while his mother was knitting it. Choice D is incorrect. After the play, his mother admitted that she was not good at knitting, but this is not when the costume split in half.

9. E: The passage begins by stating that the reason that there are different breeds of dogs is that humans needed to use animals to fill specific needs. It goes on the explain why scent hounds are good for hunting, and it ends by stating that early hunters bred the dogs to encourage their traits. Therefore, the best answer choice is Choice E. The passage is explaining one of the needs—hunting—that was filled by breeding dogs with excellent hunting abilities. Choice A is incorrect. Although the traits are described, they aren't the main purpose of the passage. These descriptions are used to demonstrate one reason why humans began to breed dogs. Choice B is incorrect. Early hunters bred dogs with certain abilities, but early hunting techniques are not discussed. Choice D is incorrect. The purpose of the passage is not to show that scent hounds are the best hunting breed. The passage does not state which breed is the best for hunting.

10. B: Things inevitably went wrong for the family and there were problems they couldn't solve on their own, and this is how they discovered that the RV community is incredibly helpful and friendly. This can also be proof that Choice C is incorrect. Choice A is incorrect. The passage never states that the family learned how to back the RV into small spaces. Choice D is incorrect. Making friends and packing up daily are both mentioned in the passage, but a connection is never made between the two. In fact, the passage states that the family made new friends. Choice E is incorrect because the passage says the family laughed when they had difficulty backing up the RV.

11. E: The RV is described as big, and the family had difficulty, or "comical attempts," to back "The Beast" into small spaces. This shows that it was very large and that it could be difficult to control, making Choice E correct. There is nothing in the passage that says the RV was scary to look at or uncomfortable to ride in, so Choices A and B are incorrect. The first sentence says that the RV was "a great purchase for our family and brought us all closer together," so Choices C and D are incorrect.

12. B: It is stated that new word combinations such as "eye hats" are interesting. They suggest an understanding of language or vocabulary. Choice A and Choice C are incorrect. Both Koko's understood

127

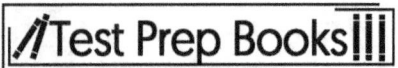

Answer Explanations

vocabulary and signed vocabulary are of interest, but the fact that she could put the two together to create language was more fascinating. Choice D is incorrect. Acquiring vocabulary requires repetition and mimicry, much like how a parrot can acquire vocabulary. As noted above, the ability to create new words based on an understanding of other words proves more interesting. Choice E is incorrect because Koko's age when she passed is not part of her communication skills.

13. C: The passages states that he has looked forward to this vacation all year, so Choice C is correct. Raul has been fascinated with pyramids since childhood, not looking forward to the vacation since childhood, so Choice A is incorrect. The word *month* is in the passage, but the context is that Raul's vacation is next month, not that he's been excited about it for a month. Therefore, Choice B is incorrect. *Many years* can be found in the passage, but this in reference to how long it has been since Raul has read about the history of the pyramids, so Choice D is incorrect. *All year* is probably longer than a few days, so Choice E is incorrect.

14. E: The text says that the Great Pyramid of Giza is a wonder of the ancient world. Specifically, it is the oldest of the Seven Wonders of the Ancient World. While the other answer choices relate to things mentioned in the text, they do not suggest the incredible age of the Great Pyramid in the same way as Choice E.

15. D: Choice D is correct because Julio broke his promise to his mother that he would clean his room. All of the other answer choices are incorrect. Nothing physical was broken in the passage.

16. C: Butterflies use a chrysalis to transform, not a cocoon. All of the other answer choices are mentioned in the passage as something both need or do.

17. E: Looking at a cocoon or chrysalis would probably not be a problem, since looking at an object does not involve touching it and is usually harmless. All other actions described would likely disturb the coverings, which the passage says not to do.

18. A: The passage describes the process of metamorphosis as the insects changing form. Choices B and C would mean the insects are taking different actions than the ones described in the passage. Choices D and E use the word as the name of a species instead, which is not correct.

19. D: The final sentence indicates that butterflies and moths need their covering to survive the changes they go through. The passage does not provide specific information about the transformation or caterpillar diets as in Choices A and B, does not give instructions for how to make caterpillars do anything as in Choice C, and does not say anything about any people as in Choice E.

20. B: The shouting in Choice B is the closest to the kind of cry described in the passage. Choice A uses another meaning of the word *cry*, which Sally is not described as doing. Choices C and E make assumptions about how Sally was feeling that are not supported by the passage. Choice D is incorrect because Sally was calling out to everyone else, not Jordan, and it is not clear if she was angry with him.

21. A: Akash is afraid that he might fall if he climbs up after Jordan. The passage specifically says that he isn't sure he believes Choice B. Choices C and D contain ideas never brought up in the passage. Choice E doesn't fit with the fact that he tells Sally to go get her mom.

22. C: Choice C offers Akash another option to try to stop Jordan from falling and hurting himself. Choice A seems more like advice for Jordan. Choice B suggests that Sally is being mean to Jordan, which the

128

Answer Explanations

passage does not indicate. Choice *D* does not help with the situation at hand. Choice *E* makes an assumption about Sally's mother that the passage gives no reason to believe is true.

23. A: The passage says that the protein *CONSTANS* starts the process. Choices *B* and *E* suggest that the cold makes flowers bloom, which is not true. Choice *C* is incorrect, as there is no indication of people giving the flowers instructions. Choice *D* is about making proteins, not the action that a certain protein kicks off.

24. D: The passage does not say how *CONSTANS* got its name. All other choices contain information stated in the passage.

25. D: The word *great* expresses an opinion about flowers in spring. Choices *A–C* all share facts, and Choice *E* confirms that a fact is true.

26. D: The passage says that the tiger has been repeatedly prevented from pouncing by the appearance of "the bigger one." Choices *A* and *C* bring up things that only happen or come up at the end of the passage. Choice *B* makes an assumption that the passage has no evidence to support. Choice *E* is incorrect because the tiger wants to eat a human, not be friends with them.

27. B: The narration indicates that the tiger does not want to put in the effort to deal with both humans. The passage specifically says that neither is a match for him, making Choice *A* the wrong answer. Choices *C* and *E* bring up ideas not mentioned in the passage. There is no implication that either human sees him, as in Choice *D*.

28. C: The passage indicates that he thinks of the boy as a low-effort snack and doesn't even think humans taste good, so Choice *C* makes the most sense to assume. There is no reason to assume that he is the only tiger in the jungle, making Choice *A* incorrect. Choices *B* and *D* rely on assumptions about the tiger's diet that the passage does not provide evidence for. Choice *E* is incorrect because the passage suggests he doesn't like the taste of humans very much.

SSAT Elementary Practice Test 3

Quantitative Section

1. Which of the following fractions is equivalent to 0.75?
    a. $\frac{1}{75}$
    b. $\frac{3}{25}$
    c. $\frac{75}{2}$
    d. $\frac{1}{4}$
    e. $\frac{3}{4}$

2. Which of the following is a factor of 27?
    a. 54
    b. 2
    c. 9
    d. 13
    e. 7

3. Find the value of $16 \times 4 - 8 \div 2$.
    a. 28
    b. 62
    c. 60
    d. 56
    e. 0

4. Round 1,458,983,239 to the nearest ten million.
    a. 1,460,000,000
    b. 1,459,000,000
    c. 1,450,000,000
    d. 1,500,000,000
    e. 1,458,000,000

5. Multiply the following: $239 \times 10,000,000,000$.
    a. 2,390,000,000
    b. 2,390,000,000,000
    c. 23,900,000,000
    d. 239,000,000,000
    e. 2,390,000,000,000

6. Which of the following is a three-dimensional shape?
   a. Circle
   b. Triangle
   c. Hexagon
   d. Cube
   e. Square

7. Trevor went to buy school supplies. He spent a total of $18.25. He bought 3 notebooks, 2 packages of paper, and 1 pencil sharpener. How many boxes of pens did he buy?

Item	Cost
Notebook	$2.75
Package of paper	$1.50
Pencil sharpener	$3.00
Box of pens	$2.00

   a. 2
   b. 3
   c. 4
   d. 5
   e. 6

8. The basketball team is hosting a bake sale to raise money for new uniforms. They want to make sure they have enough desserts to sell. If there are 13 players on the team and the coach asks everyone to make two dozen cookies or brownies to sell, how many cookies and brownies will there be for sale at the bake sale?
   a. 26
   b. 156
   c. 624
   d. 312
   e. 338

9. Melody is in the grocery store with her mother. She is trying to estimate how much the groceries will cost. If her mother buys the following items, what is the estimated total cost, rounded to the nearest dollar?

   2 gallons of milk: $3.57 each
   Half a dozen oranges: $6.00 per dozen
   2 pounds of apples: $1.58 per pound
   Cereal: $4.28
   Bread: $2.73

   a. $22
   b. $18
   c. $25
   d. $23
   e. $16

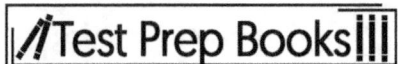

10. Matthew's grandmother gave him $10.00 to spend on anything he wants at the store, but he can't decide what to buy. His choices are anime trading cards ($5.69 per pack), candy bars ($1.59 each), a baseball ($7.99), and a box of sidewalk chalk ($4.25). If there are no other costs, which combination of items comes closest to $10.00 without going over?
    a. The trading cards and two candy bars
    b. The trading cards and the sidewalk chalk
    c. The baseball and two candy bars
    d. The sidewalk chalk and four candy bars
    e. Two packs of trading cards

11. The deer and rabbits have been feasting on Sophia's prized flowers! She is very upset and has decided that she must put a fence around her entire flower garden. Her flower garden is a square that is 18 feet on each side. How many feet of fencing will she need to enclose the whole garden?
    a. 90
    b. 324
    c. 36
    d. 54
    e. 72

12. Jill, Kai, Jayden, and Alex were having a race to see who could do the most math problems in 30 minutes. According to the graph below, who completed the most problems?

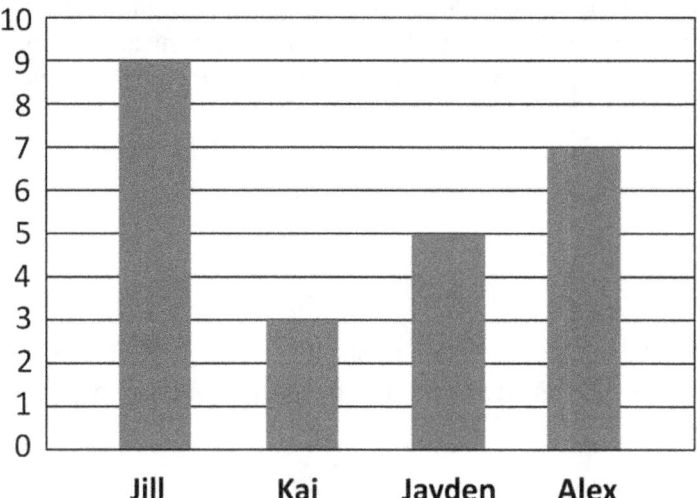

    a. Jill
    b. Kai
    c. Jayden
    d. Alex
    e. It was a tie.

13. Four basketball teams competed in the final playoff games. Together, the teams scored 350 points. The teams with the top two scores will get to play in the championship game. According to the bar graph, which two teams will be playing against each other?

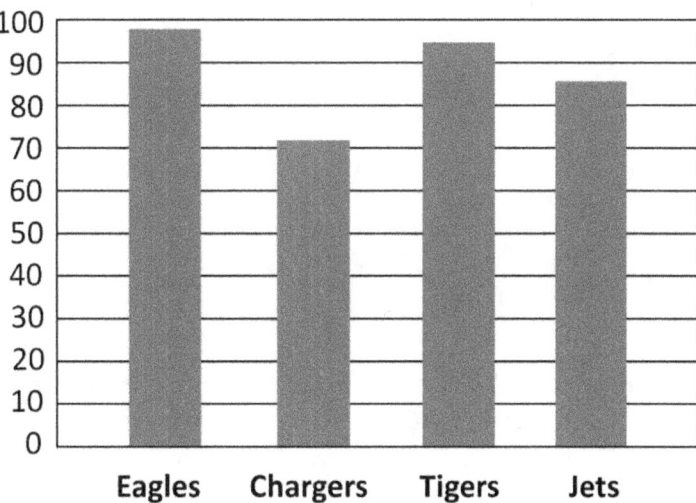

a. Jets vs. Chargers
b. Eagles vs. Chargers
c. Chargers vs. Tigers
d. Tigers vs. Jets
e. Eagles vs. Tigers

14. Mr. Jones has to write 90 questions for his students' math tests. If he writes $\frac{1}{6}$ of the questions per day, how many questions will he have finished by the end of the third day?

a. 15
b. 6
c. 45
d. 90
e. 18

15. Toby's fifth-grade class is learning how to find equivalent forms of fractions. His teacher, Ms. Robinson, wrote the fraction $\frac{12}{200}$ on the board and asked the class to list four equivalent fractions. Which of the following would NOT be a correct answer?

a. $\frac{12}{50}$

b. $\frac{6}{100}$

c. $\frac{24}{400}$

d. $\frac{3}{50}$

e. $\frac{30}{500}$

16. Mrs. Abrams's class is having a lot of trouble coming in from the playground on time. Of her 28 students, 5 took too long taking their coats off and getting to their desks, 4 stopped at the water fountain on the way back to the classroom, and 2 went to use the restroom. What fraction of the students were late because they went to get water?
    a. $\frac{2}{28}$
    b. $\frac{1}{7}$
    c. $\frac{4}{14}$
    d. $\frac{11}{28}$
    e. $\frac{17}{28}$

17. Chase's mother asked him to go to the store and buy a few things. The groceries cost $26, and Chase got $14 back in change. How much money did Chase's mother give him to go to the store?
    a. $14
    b. $26
    c. $12
    d. $40
    e. $30

18. Frank, Josie, and Larry are going to drive to the beach for the day. They decided to share the driving. The beach is 62 miles away from Frank's house, and Josie and Larry's house is on the way. Frank drove 5 miles to Josie and Larry's house, and then the three of them split the remaining driving equally. How many miles did they each drive?
    a. 19
    b. 20.67
    c. 25.67
    d. Frank = 15.67; Josie = 20.67; Larry = 20.67
    e. Frank = 24; Josie = 19; Larry = 19

19. Joshua had 90 minutes to complete a project for his boss at work. After he had been working for x minutes, his boss came in and told him that he only had 25 minutes left. How long had Joshua been working on the project when his boss came in?
    a. 115 minutes
    b. 65 minutes
    c. 75 minutes
    d. 60 minutes
    e. 90 minutes

20. Mandy has two boards that are both 14 feet long. She has cut the boards to make 3 shelves of the same size from each board. How long was each of the six shelves (in feet), and how much wood does she have left over?
   a. 4 feet; 4 feet left over
   b. 3 feet; 1 foot left over
   c. 5 feet; 2 feet left over
   d. 6 feet; no wood left over
   e. 6 feet; 4 feet left over

21. The town of Orchard Park is planning to put in a new park near the edge of town. The town planners have published a drawing of the plans for the park for all of the citizens to see.

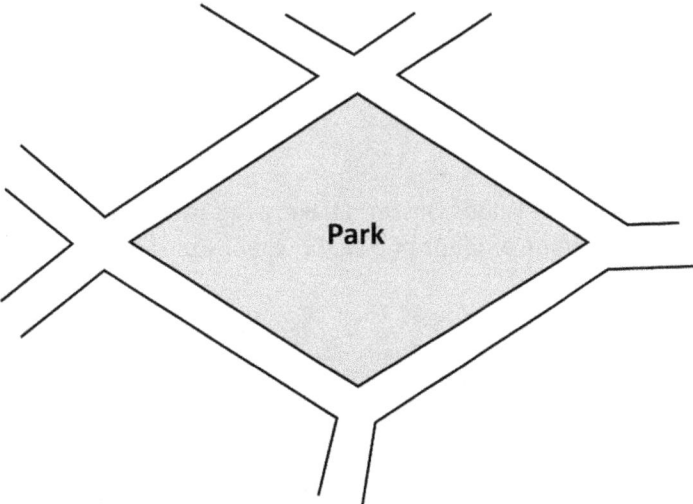

Liam and his friends are trying to decide what shape the park looks like. Liam thinks it's a square. Olivia is pretty sure it's a rhombus, but Emma thinks it's more like a rectangle. Noah says it is definitely a trapezoid. Who is right?
   a. Liam
   b. Olivia
   c. Emma
   d. Noah
   e. None of them are correct.

22. Ms. O'Brien's class is learning about symmetry. She explained that many of the letters in the alphabet are symmetrical, especially when they are written in capital letters. The students are guessing words that have all symmetrical letters. Which of the following guesses is correct?
   a. HAM
   b. TOP
   c. BALL
   d. TOYS
   e. CORD

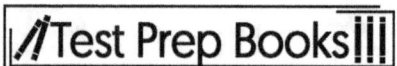

23. David, Aidan, Marian, and Ellen are working on their math homework. One of the problems is to write 93,567 in expanded form. David wrote $90000 + 3000 + 500 + 60 + 7$. Aidan wrote $(9 \times 10,000) + (3 \times 1000) + (5 \times 100) + (6 \times 10) + (7 \times 1)$. Marian wrote $93,000 + 500 + 67$. Ellen wrote $(93 \times 1000) + (56 \times 10) + (7 \times 1)$. Who got the problem correct?
   a. David
   b. David and Aidan
   c. Marian and Ellen
   d. Ellen
   e. Marian and Aidan

24. Kevin and his sister have a combined age of 16. If Kevin is 7 years old, how old is his sister?
   a. 10
   b. 16
   c. 8
   d. 7
   e. 9

25. There were 21 pies for sale at Delicious Desserts bakery this morning. If there were 3 bakers working, and they all made the same amount of pies, how many pies did each person bake?
   a. 3
   b. 21
   c. 7
   d. 63
   e. 5

26. Melissa is 12 years old, which is 2 years older than her little sister, Betsy. Their cousin James is twice Betsy's age. How old is James?
   a. 20
   b. 24
   c. 22
   d. 28
   e. 26

27. Which type of triangle has three angles that all measure 60 degrees?
   a. Acute and equilateral
   b. Right and scalene
   c. Obtuse and equilateral
   d. Acute and isosceles
   e. Obtuse and isosceles

28. The preschool classroom has lots of toys for the children to play with. While Amelia's mom was picking up her little brother, Amelia was looking at the toys and deciding which 3-dimensional shape they represented. The ball was easy, and so were the blocks, but she had some trouble with a strange toy that had triangular ends and three flat parallelogram sides. What is this shape?
   a. Square prism
   b. Square pyramid
   c. Triangular pyramid
   d. Triangular prism

e. Rectangular prism

29. Oliver is helping his mother put away groceries. He is practicing his geometry while he helps, identifying the shape of each item. So far, he has put away a box of tissues, a can of soup, a box of cookies, a ball for his little sister, and a bag of potato chips. Which item is the cylinder?
   a. Tissue box
   b. Bag of chips
   c. Ball
   d. Box of cookies
   e. Can of soup

30. Jasmine needs to be in bed by 10:00 pm. If she needs 15 minutes to get a shower and 10 minutes to brush her teeth and hair, what time does Jasmine need to start getting ready for bed?
   a. 9:45 am
   b. 10:25 pm
   c. 9:45 pm
   d. 9:35 pm
   e. 9:55 pm

Verbal Section

Synonyms

Each of the questions below has one word, followed by five other words. Please select one answer whose meaning is closest to the word in capital letters.

1. VIVID
   a. Generic
   b. Intense
   c. Maddening
   d. Suave
   e. Tedious

2. PEDESTRIAN
   a. Conductor
   b. Driver
   c. Pilot
   d. Automobile
   e. Walker

3. AROMA
   a. Distant
   b. Distinct
   c. Horror
   d. Odor
   e. Sound

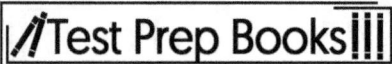

4. LEGENDARY
    a. Cynical
    b. Judicial
    c. Mythical
    d. Typical
    e. Anonymous

5. RUIN
    a. Build
    b. Idolize
    c. Transform
    d. Reconstruct
    e. Destroy

6. MANUFACTURE
    a. Disrupt
    b. Produce
    c. Recognize
    d. Trigger
    e. Count

7. HOIST
    a. Attach
    b. Hamper
    c. Lower
    d. Volunteer
    e. Lift

8. BANQUET
    a. Announcement
    b. Castle
    c. Feast
    d. Rug
    e. Silverware

9. INDUSTRIOUS
    a. Adventurous
    b. Hardworking
    c. Resistant
    d. Smart
    e. Lazy

10. VACANT
    a. Related
    b. Implied
    c. Missing
    d. Unsure
    e. Empty

11. OUTSKIRTS
    a. Boundary
    b. Oasis
    c. Metropolitan
    d. Reservoir
    e. Central

12. SELDOM
    a. Conventional
    b. Egotistical
    c. Rarely
    d. Sleepy
    e. Often

13. THRIFTY
    a. Economical
    b. Pleasant
    c. Practical
    d. Sneaky
    e. Likely

14. FLIMSY
    a. Amusing
    b. Convenient
    c. Rowdy
    d. Thin
    e. Solid

15. COAX
    a. Despise
    b. Harm
    c. Persuade
    d. Trouble
    e. Advance

Analogies

The questions below ask you to find relationships between words. For each question, select the answer that best completes the meaning of the sentence.

16. Pot is to boil as:
    a. Rope is to climb
    b. Water is to faucet
    c. Chef is to cook
    d. Mirror is to reflection
    e. Temper is to rage

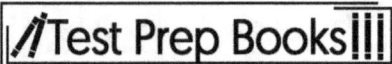

17. Hydrogen is to element as:
    a. Species is to canine
    b. Valley is to river
    c. Crayon is to elementary
    d. Project is to brand
    e. Calico is to cat

18. Small is to miniscule as:
    a. Chagrin is to elusive
    b. Confined is to rotten
    c. Unhealthy is to ailing
    d. Tall is to short
    e. Cough is to allergy

19. Mountain is to peak as wave is to:
    a. Ocean
    b. Surf
    c. Fountain
    d. Wavelength
    e. Crest

20. Flour is to cake as:
    a. Spoon is to soup
    b. Oven is to casserole
    c. Yeast is to bread
    d. Salad is to lettuce
    e. Hot fudge is to ice cream

21. Grief is to sadness as:
    a. Celebration is to birthday
    b. Merriment is to happiness
    c. Vexation is to reconciliation
    d. Tears are to crying
    e. Joy is to emotion

22. Doctor is to stethoscope as:
    a. Book is to teacher
    b. Nurse is to hospital
    c. Pipes are to plumber
    d. Sculptor is to museum
    e. Carpenter is to hammer

23. Green is to color as:
    a. Mammal is to animal
    b. Mammal is to dog
    c. Purple is to violet
    d. Appliance is to kitchen
    e. Color spectrum is to rainbow

24. Pencil is to write as soap is to:
    a. Bubble
    b. Cleanse
    c. Scrub
    d. Rinse
    e. Shower

25. Golden Retriever is to dog as:
    a. Bottlenose Dolphin is to fish
    b. Cat is to Siamese
    c. American Quarter Horse is to horse
    d. Snake is to cobra
    e. Child is to human

26. Brake is to stop as:
    a. Food is to hydrate
    b. Promise is to pledge
    c. Deer is to hunt
    d. Tape is to adhesive
    e. Money is to purchase

27. Love is to red as royalty is to:
    a. Purple
    b. Crown
    c. Gold
    d. Scepter
    e. Silver

28. Pair is to pear as:
    a. Hair is to there
    b. To is to through
    c. Can't is to cannot
    d. Stair is to stare
    e. Fair is to fear

29. Hungry is to famished as angry is to:
    a. Upset
    b. Irritated
    c. Irate
    d. Annoyed
    e. Hatred

30. Chapter is to novel as:
    a. Whisper is to silence
    b. Tangle is to lengthening
    c. Poem is to poet
    d. Feeling is to past
    e. Brushstroke is to painting

Reading Section

Read the following passage, and then answer questions 1-3.

Laura's mother always told her that she was growing like a weed, but Laura wasn't sure she believed her. She felt like she would be the shrimpy little sister who couldn't reach things for the rest of her life. Johnny didn't help, always grabbing things out of her hands and holding them high over his head where she couldn't reach, even by jumping.

That was why Laura had to try on those shoes. She wasn't being naughty, just practical. They weren't doing anyone any good languishing in the back of the closet anyway. Everything would have been fine if she hadn't gotten caught—she could tell it was a problem that she couldn't balance in them, so she would have put them right back, but her mother simply wouldn't believe her no matter how hard she tried to explain. She didn't belong in the corner! It was so unfair.

1. What does the word *languishing* mean in this passage?
    a. Sparkling
    b. Falling down
    c. Being useful
    d. Being wasted
    e. Getting smaller

2. How is Laura feeling, based on how the passage is narrated?
    a. Annoyed that Johnny was never punished
    b. Pleased that she got to try on the shoes
    c. Resentful of the punishment she has received
    d. Relieved to still be small enough to sneak into places
    e. Ready to seek revenge on her mother for punishing her

3. Why would Laura have put the shoes back in the closet?
    a. She had gotten them there in the first place.
    b. Her mother had told her to put them there.
    c. Johnny wouldn't be able to find them there.
    d. She didn't want anyone to know where they were.
    e. She was unable to balance when she tried them on.

Read the following passage, and then answer questions 4-7.

A puppy has no idea that it's done something wrong if it isn't taught by its owner. It is an animal, after all, and what's more, it's only a baby. It has very little experience with the world and how it works to live among humans. If you make the choice to bring a puppy home, it's important that you understand that you have made a commitment to raise that puppy to be a well-behaved full-grown dog. It will certainly need to be fed and taken on walks, as you likely already know, but it will also need training and discipline. As the person responsible for your new dog's well-being, you must be able to handle these things.

SSAT Elementary Practice Test 3

4. What is the main idea of this passage?
   a. Puppies are adorable and have no clue what's going on.
   b. Raising a puppy is a big responsibility to take on.
   c. Everyone knows to feed and walk a dog if they have one.
   d. Dogs are always well-behaved once they reach their adult size.
   e. Puppies are animals and babies.

5. Which of these is NOT a reason the passage gives that a puppy may misbehave?
   a. It is too young to understand what it means to misbehave.
   b. Animals do not have human understanding of right and wrong.
   c. Puppies can get angry with their humans and may want to do wrong.
   d. Puppies need to be trained by their owners.
   e. It is the dog owner's responsibility to handle these things.

6. Which of these would the passage's writer probably say is most important to do?
   a. Pick the right puppy to take home
   b. Give the puppy a good name
   c. Walk the puppy at least a mile every day
   d. Train the puppy so it knows how to behave
   e. Feed the puppy a balanced diet, including eggs and grains

7. What is the most likely reason the passage's author chose to write about this topic?
   a. The author really likes dogs and wants to tell people about them.
   b. The author thinks nobody is raising their puppies right and is angry about it.
   c. The author wants to make sure people remember certain important parts of puppy care.
   d. The author hates dogs and wants people to stop adopting them.
   e. The author is afraid of dogs and wants them to go away.

Read the following passage, and then answer questions 8-11.

> Grayson and Vanessa used to be very good friends. Grayson would even share his favorite food with Vanessa's little sister, Ellie. He didn't like to part with any of his fruit snacks, the grape-flavored ones especially, but Vanessa and Ellie could always have one if they asked, though he did hope they didn't ask for grape.
>
> Everything was great until the day *somebody* pushed Grayson off the monkey bars. The force of the fall took the wind out of Grayson's lungs, and it hurt so much, but nobody saw! That nasty Tim Winston was going to get away with it! Grayson still had tears in his eyes when he picked up a rock from the edge of the playground and threw it at Tim's head. His aim was off, and the rock hit Ellie. Neither sister talks to Grayson anymore.

8. What was special about Grayson's fruit snacks?
   a. They were all grape flavored.
   b. They included grape-flavored ones.
   c. They made Grayson more friends.
   d. They were the only food he shared with Ellie.
   e. They were Grayson's favorite food.

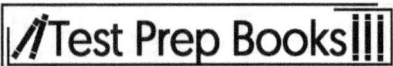

SSAT Elementary Practice Test 3

9. Why did Grayson share his fruit snacks with Ellie?
    a. Grayson was nice to Ellie because of his friendship with Vanessa.
    b. Ellie was Grayson's best friend before the rock incident happened.
    c. Ellie wouldn't take no for an answer when she wanted one.
    d. Ellie asked very nicely, so he felt like he should share some.
    e. Vanessa made Grayson share because they were friends.

10. Which of these might help Grayson become friends with the sisters again?
    a. If a teacher had been outside on the playground the day Grayson threw the rock
    b. If Grayson offered the sisters a heartfelt apology for throwing the rock
    c. If Ellie and Vanessa were nicer people than they are in the story
    d. If Grayson had picked a dirt clod instead of a rock to throw at Tim Winston
    e. If Grayson had deliberately thrown the rock at Ellie

11. Which of the following is true about Tim Winston in the passage?
    a. He is the only person in the school who has a last name.
    b. He is mentioned before shoving Grayson on the monkey bars.
    c. He pushed multiple children the day he pushed Grayson.
    d. The passage does not give a reason why he would have pushed Grayson.
    e. The passage says that Grayson is the worst bully in the school.

Read the following passage, and then answer questions 12-15.

> George Washington was the first president of the United States, from 1789 to 1797. Washington had very strong feelings about one person having the kind of power that a position like the presidency offered, and he stepped down after two four-year terms in office so that he would not hold this power for too long. He also felt that political parties would be harmful to the budding nation and wanted the United States to continue having none.

12. What does *terms* mean in the passage?
    a. Pieces of silver
    b. Vocabulary words
    c. Periods of time
    d. Dishes
    e. Papers

13. Which of these things would bother George Washington the most based on information in this passage?
    a. Seeing how much of politics in the United States is based on political parties now
    b. Knowing that there are countries in the world where presidents serve longer terms
    c. People forgetting his name and the position that he held in this country
    d. The length of a presidential term being changed to five years instead of four
    e. Finding out how many presidents there have been since he was in office

144

SSAT Elementary Practice Test 3

14. Why did George Washinton step down as president in 1797?
    a. He was just tired of the work of being the president of a whole country.
    b. He disapproved of one person holding that power too long, even himself.
    c. He thought that people would get mad at him if he stayed in office too long.
    d. He disliked the political party system that would keep him in office longer.
    e. He wanted to rule something else now.

15. Which of the following does this passage indicate?
    a. That George Washington did not approve of political parties
    b. That the power of the presidency automatically corrupts those who hold it
    c. That George Washington chopped down a cherry tree
    d. That presidents serve for two four-year terms each
    e. That George Washington hated being president

Read the following passage, and answer the question below.

> Technology has been invading cars for the last several years, but there are some new high-tech trends that are pretty amazing. It is now standard in many car models to have a rear-view camera, hands-free phone and text, and a touch screen digital display. Music can be streamed from a paired cell phone, and most displays can even be programmed with a personal photo. Sensors beep to indicate there is something in the driver's path when reversing and changing lanes. Rain-sensing windshield wipers and lights are automatic, leaving the driver with little to do but watch the road and enjoy the ride. The next wave of technology will include cars that automatically parallel park, and self-driving cars are on the horizon. These technological advances make it a good time to be a driver.

16. Based on the passage, which of the following can be concluded?
    a. Technology will continue to influence how cars are made.
    b. Windshield wipers and lights are always automatic.
    c. It is standard to have a rear-view camera in all cars.
    d. Technology has reached its peak in cars.
    e. Technology will never replace human drivers.

Read the following passage, and answer the question below.

> Proponents of humanities education are starting to push back in the face of both budget and faculty cuts. With STEM subjects (science, technology, engineering and mathematics) and professors bringing in more grant money to research universities, it's easy to see why many of them feel as if they're fighting an uphill battle.

17. What is implied in this passage?
    a. More students take STEM classes than humanities courses.
    b. Research universities invest in fields that bring in grants.
    c. Humanities professors need to bring in more grant money.
    d. STEM is more valuable than humanities.
    e. Humanities education does not have a future at universities.

Read the following passage, and answer the question below.

> Predators are animals that eat other animals. Prey are animals that are eaten by a predator. Predators and prey have a distinct relationship. Predators rely on the prey population for food and nutrition. The prey population may develop features that allow them to escape and hide from their predators.

18. If a cat is a predator and a mouse is its prey, which of the following is true?
    a. Cats are eaten by mice.
    b. Cats have developed features that allow them to escape from mice.
    c. Cats rely on mice for food and nutrition.
    d. Cats and mice have an extinct relationship.
    e. Cats and mice have no relationship.

Read the following passage, and answer the question below.

> Invasive species, both plants and animals, tend to crowd out native species, utilizing or depleting the resources they need to survive. In some cases, such as Burmese pythons in the Everglades, they become the apex predator at the top of the food chain, leading to a significant decline in several native animal species.

19. What do invasive species do?
    a. Exist alongside native species
    b. Form symbiotic relationships
    c. Crowd out native species
    d. Starve due to non-native conditions
    e. Create new resources that help native species

Read the following passage, and answer the question below.

> Home improvement projects can be pricey, but there are ways to keep costs down such as "Do It Yourself," or DIY; comparing prices of the materials and workers that will be used; and keeping the original layout for plumbing pipes and electrical wires.

20. What is the subject of this sentence?
    a. DIY home improvement
    b. Where to buy construction supplies
    c. Comparing the cost of workers and materials
    d. Plumbing and electrical layout
    e. Keeping costs of home improvement down

Read the following passage, and answer the question below.

> Asbestos was a dangerous yet popular product, widely produced for over one hundred years. Due to its durability and fire resistance, it was used in a wide range of products, such as houses, cars, and ships. As with tobacco, evidence was presented early on that asbestos was dangerous and had cumulative adverse effects, but production didn't decline until the 1970s.

21. When did production of asbestos decrease?
    a. One hundred years ago
    b. When evidence was presented that it was dangerous
    c. When it was no longer durable
    d. In the 1970s
    e. Within the last ten years

Read the following passage, and answer the question below.

> Asteroids and comets are thought to be leftover parts from the same giant cloud of gas and dust that condensed to create the Sun, planets, and moons about 4.5 billion years ago. Some people even theorize that the main asteroids, which lie in a tight belt between Mars and Jupiter, may all be fragments from another planet that was forming there that suffered some sort of major collision and broke into thousands of little pieces.

22. Which of the following are theorized to be a result of a major collision that caused a planet to break into thousands of pieces?
    a. The Sun, planets, and moons
    b. Mars and Jupiter
    c. Earth
    d. Comets
    e. The main asteroids that are found between Mars and Jupiter

Read the following passage, and answer the question below.

> A medical condition called "osteoporosis" happens when the body loses bone or makes too little bone tissue. This can lead to brittle, fragile bones that easily break. Bones are already porous (meaning they have small holes), and when osteoporosis sets in, the spaces in bones become much larger, causing the bones to weaken. Both men and women can develop osteoporosis, though it is most common in women over age 50. Loss of bone can be silent and increase over time, so it is important to be take action in prevention of the disease.

23. What is the main purpose of this passage?
    a. To discuss some of the ways people contract osteoporosis
    b. To describe different treatment options for those with osteoporosis
    c. To explain how to prevent osteoporosis
    d. To define osteoporosis
    e. To teach readers about how bones work

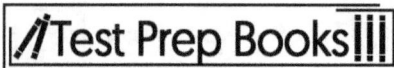

Read the following passage, and answer the question below.

> Jason had never been the best student. He had failed three math tests and turned in only half of his homework. Worrying about his graduation, Jason's mother signed him up for tutoring. Even after several sessions, it was unclear whether he would pass. In the last week of math class, Jason worked hard and passed. Jason's math teacher was impressed at his improvement.

24. When did Jason begin to show improvement?
    a. After half of his tutoring sessions.
    b. After his last tutoring session.
    c. This cannot be determined.
    d. During the last week of class.
    e. When he began his tutoring sessions.

Read the following passage, and then answer questions 25-28.

> If you're being paid to play baseball, then you're doing it professionally. Most people are aware of this fact, and many also know that the Major Leagues are not the only ones paying players: There is a Minor League system as well. But how many are aware of the system that divides the Minor League into classes?
>
> There are five classes in the Minor League system. Triple-A (AAA) is the highest class of Minor League baseball, followed by Double-A (AA), Class A/Single-A (A), Class A Short Season, and Rookie. All of these levels are paid, but the minimum salary for each level is different, with the Rookies receiving the least, then Class A Short Season receiving more, then Single-A, then Double-A, and then Triple-A players receiving the most.

25. What does the passage writer most likely think about the average person's knowledge of the Minor League system in baseball?
    a. People are more likely than not to know what all the Minor League levels are.
    b. People are not highly likely to know what all the levels in the Minor League system are.
    c. People generally know more about the Minor Leagues than they do about the Major Leagues.
    d. People only know anything at all about the Minor Leagues if they play baseball themselves.
    e. Nobody knows anything about the Minor League system.

26. Which of the following statements is true?
    a. Rookies receive more pay than Class A players.
    b. Double-A players receive more pay than Triple-A players.
    c. Double-A players receive less pay than Triple-A players.
    d. Triple-A players receive less pay than Double-A players.
    e. Single-A players receive more pay than Rookies.

27. According to the passage, which of the Minor Leagues contain professional baseball players?
   a. None of the minor leagues contain professionals because only the Major League players are professionals.
   b. Every class above Class A Short Season has professional players.
   c. All are paid, so all are professional baseball players.
   d. None are paid, so none are professional baseball players.
   e. Who is viewed as professional depends on the year.

28. What are the different levels of Minor League baseball called?
   a. Classes
   b. Steps
   c. Echelons
   d. Players
   e. Games

Writing Sample

Tell a story using the picture below. Make sure that your story has a beginning, middle, and end.

The following pages are provided for writing your story.

Answer Explanations

Quantitative Section

1. E: To find the fraction form of 0.75, write 75 over 100. We use 100 since the 5 is in the hundredth place. Then, reduce the fraction by dividing both the numerator and denominator by 25. The answer is $\frac{75}{100} = \frac{3}{4}$.

2. C: A factor of a number is a number that can be divided into the given value without a remainder. $27 \div 9 = 3$, so, 9 is a factor of 27. 54 is a multiple of 27. 2, 7, and 13 are neither factors nor multiples.

3. C: Order of operations must be followed. Therefore, perform the multiplication and division first from left to right to obtain $64 - 4$. Then, perform the subtraction to obtain a result of 60.

4. A: The value in the ten million place is 5. The value to its right is an 8, which is greater than (or equal to) 5. Therefore, we round the 5 up to a 6 and the rest of the values to the right become zeros. The correct answer is 1,460,000,000.

5. B: To multiply by a multiple of 10, count the number of zeros in the multiple of ten. In this case, there are 10 zeros in 10,000,000,000. Then, attach them to the right of 239. The correct answer is 2,390,000,000,000.

6. D: A cube is a three-dimensional solid shape. Two-dimensional shapes are flat like circles, triangles, hexagons, squares, and other similar shapes.

7. A: Trevor bought 2 boxes of pens. If he bought 3 notebooks, 2 packages of paper, and 1 pencil sharpener, then he spent $8.25, $3, and $3 on those items respectively. The total of those items then is $14.25. The difference between the total of those items and the total spent of $18.25 is $4. Therefore, he bought 2 boxes of pens at $2 apiece for $4.

8. D: Two dozen means each player has to make 24 cookies or brownies; 13 players times 24 equals 312 cookies and brownies for the bake sale. Choice A multiplies by 2 rather than by two dozen. Choice B multiplies by one dozen rather than two, and Choice C multiplies by two dozen cookies AND two dozen brownies, which would be a lot of treats. Choice E incorrectly interprets a dozen as 13 (which is sometimes known as a *baker's dozen*).

9. A: A gallon of milk rounds up to $4 per gallon, so 2 gallons would be $8. The oranges are $6 per dozen, but her mother is only buying half a dozen, which would be $3. Rounding the apples up to $2 per pound means that 2 pounds would be approximately $4. The cost of the cereal rounds down to $4, and the cost of the bread rounds up to $3. If we add the numbers together, we get $8 + $3 + $4 + $4 + $3, which equals $22. The answer for Choice B forgets that Mom bought 2 gallons of milk, and Choice C counted a full dozen of oranges rather than half a dozen. Choice D rounded the cereal up rather than down to the nearest dollar. Choice E only counts one of every item instead of 2 gallons of milk and 2 pounds of apples.

10. B: The anime trading cards plus the box of sidewalk chalk totals $9.94. Choice A, the trading cards plus two candy bars, adds up to $8.87. Choice C, the baseball plus two candy bars, is too expensive at

Answer Explanations

$11.17. Choice D, the sidewalk chalk plus the baseball, is too much at $12.24. Choice E, two packs of trading cards, is too expensive at $11.38.

11. E: To find the perimeter of a space, add the length of each side: $18 + 18 + 18 + 18 = 72$ ft. Choice A multiplied the length five times instead of four. Choice B multiplied the length times the width, which would give the area of the garden rather than the perimeter. Choice C added the length and width of two sides but did not account for fencing on all four sides of the space. Choice D added three sides instead of all four.

12. A: The graph shows that Jill completed 9 problems, which is the most of the four friends. Alex, Choice D, completed the next highest number of problems, followed by Jayden, Choice C. Kai, Choice B, had the lowest number at 3.

13. E: The Eagles and the Tigers had the two highest scores (98 and 94), so they will compete in the championship game. Choice A shows the two teams with the lowest scores. Although Choice B does show the Eagles, who had the highest score, the Chargers had the lowest score and will not be in the game. Choice D includes the Tigers, but wrongly includes the Chargers. Choice D shows the two teams that scored in the middle of the four teams.

14. C: $\frac{1}{6}$ of 90 questions is 15 questions per day (90 divided by 6). By the end of the third day, Mr. Jones will have written 15×3 questions, or 45 questions. Choice A is the number of questions he writes each day, and Choice B is the total number of days it will take him to write all the questions. Choice D is the total number of questions he has to write. Choice E multiplies 6 questions by 3 days.

15. A: $\frac{12}{50}$ reduces the denominator by 4 but does not also reduce the numerator by the same amount. Choices B and D both reduce the fraction. Choice C multiplies the numerator and denominator by 2 and Choice E multiplies the numerator and denominator by 2.5, which also create equivalent fractions.

16. B: To find the fraction, write the number of students who went for water over the total students: $\frac{4}{28}$. Then, reduce that to its lowest form by dividing the numerator and denominator by 4: $\frac{1}{7}$. Choice A is almost correct, but it instead counts the students who were late because of using the restroom, and it does not reduce the fraction. Choice C reduces the denominator but not the numerator. Choice D counts all the students who were late instead of only those getting water, and Choice E counts all of the students who were not late.

17. D: The unknown number for this equation is how much money Chase started with. To solve this problem, set up the equation as x minus the cost of the groceries equals the change Chase got back, or $x - 26 = 14$. Choices A and B are factors already given in the problem rather than the solution to the missing number. Choice C subtracts 14 from 26 rather than adding 14 to 26. Choice E incorrectly adds $26 and $14.

18. E: To solve this problem, first subtract the 5 miles that Frank drove from the total. Then, divide the remaining miles by 3. The equation looks like this: $\frac{62-5}{3}$. First, solve the top of the equation by completing the subtraction: $62 - 5 = 57$. Then, divide $57 \div 3 = 19$. This means that Josie and Larry each drove 19 miles and Frank drove 24 miles (19 + the first 5 miles he drove to their house). Choice A does not include the extra 5 miles Frank drove to pick up Josie and Larry. Choice B has them all driving the same number of miles from the start rather than Frank driving the first 5 miles alone. Choice C is like

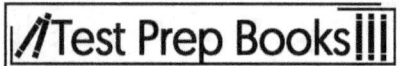

Answer Explanations

Choice *B*, but it adds five additional miles. Choice *D* subtracts the first 5 miles before dividing but then subtracts it again from Frank's total.

19. B: The equation to solve this problem is $x + 25 = 90$, where x is how long Joshua had been working and 25 minutes is how long he had left. To solve the problem, subtract 25 from both sides of the equation: $x = 90 - 25$. Choice *A* adds 25 minutes to the equation rather than subtracting it. Choices *C* and *D* are just errors in subtraction, and Choice *E* does not subtract anything from the total time.

20. A: The first step is to find out how long each shelf was. We know she made 3 shelves of equal length (x) from each board, so: $3x = 14$. Divide 14 by 3 to get $x = 4$ with a remainder of 2 feet. That's for one board. If she did that for two boards, she made 6 shelves of 4 feet each and had 4 feet of wood left over.

21. B: Olivia is correct because a rhombus is a four-sided figure where the opposite sides are parallel. Liam's guess of a square, Choice *A*, is a four-sided figure, but a square has four equal and parallel sides with four right angles. Similarly, Emma's choice of a rectangle, Choice *C*, has four sides and four right angles, but only the opposite sides are congruent. In a trapezoid, Choice *D*, only one set of the lines is parallel, and there are no right angles.

22. A: Symmetry means that two sides of the figure are mirror images of each other. The word HAM includes three symmetrical letters: H, A, and M. A vertical line can be drawn down the middle of each letter, and the two halves will be identical. Choice *B* has two symmetrical letters, but the letter P is not symmetrical. The letter B in Choice *C* has a horizontal line of symmetry, and the letter A has a vertical line of symmetry; however, the letter L is not symmetrical. In Choice *D*, the letters T, O, and Y are symmetrical, but the letter S is not. In Choice *E*, the letters C, O, and D are vertically symmetrical, but R is not.

23. B: David and Aidan are both correct. David used expanded notation, whereas Aidan used expanded factors. David is not the only one who is correct, Choice *A*. Marian and Ellen, Choices *C* and *D*, both only wrote it in partially expanded form.

24. E: The equation for this problem is $7 + x = 16$. Subtract 7 from both sides to get $x = 9$.

25. C: The equation here is the number of bakers times an unknown number of pies equals 21, or $3x = 21$. To solve this, divide both sides by 3, so $x = 7$. Each person baked 7 pies. Choice *A* is the number of bakers rather than the number of pies they made, and Choice *B* is the total number of pies rather than how much each person made. Choice *D* multiplies by 3 rather than dividing by 3. Choice *E* incorrectly divides the total pies.

26. A: Melissa is 12, Betsy's age is $12 - 2$, and James's age is $(12 - 2) \times 2$, so the equation to solve this problem is $(12 - 2) \times 2 = x$. Using PEMDAS for the order of operations, first solve what is inside the parentheses, which will make the new equation $10 \times 2 = x$. James is 20 years old. Choice *B* is twice Melissa's age rather than Betsy's, and Choice *C* adds the sisters' ages together. Choice *D* adds 2 years for Betsy's age rather than subtracting 2 years. Choice *E* doubles Melissa's age, then adds 2 years.

27. A: An acute triangle is a triangle in which all angles measure less than 90 degrees. Since this triangle has three acute angles that are all equal, it is both acute and equilateral. A right triangle has one angle that is 90 degrees, Choice *B*, and a scalene triangle has no congruent sides. An obtuse triangle, Choices *C* and *E*, has one angle greater than 90 degrees, and an isosceles triangle, Choices *D* and *E*, has two congruent sides.

Answer Explanations

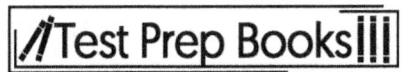

28. D: A triangular prism has triangular ends and flat sides. A square prism, Choice *A*, has four sides and squares at the ends. A pyramid, Choices *B* and *C*, has sides that rise to an apex, or a point, rather than having parallelogram sides. A rectangular prism, Choice *E*, has four sides and squares at the end.

29. E: A cylinder has two circular ends and one curved face, such as a can of soup. The tissue box, Choice *A*, is a polygon, either a cube or cuboid (depending on which type of tissues Oliver's mom likes to buy). The chips, Choice *B*, come in a bag, which is an irregular cuboid due to the closed ends. The ball, Choice *C*, is a sphere. The box of cookies, like the tissue box, is likely cuboid.

30. D: To solve this problem, subtract the time Jasmine needs from her 10:00 pm bedtime. To get a shower, she would need to start at 9:45 (15 minutes before 10:00). To brush her teeth and hair, she needs another 10 minutes, which means she needs to start getting ready for bed by 9:35. Choice *A* mixes up am (morning) and pm (evening), and incorrectly does the math. Choice *B* adds the time rather than subtracting it, making Jasmine late for bed. Choice *C* only accounts for her shower but not brushing her teeth and hair. Choice *E* subtracts the 10 minutes from the 15 minutes, implying Jasmine will get ready for bed in just 5 minutes.

Verbal Section

Synonyms

1. B: *Vivid* is an adjective that means visually striking, and it's also used to describe something that is intense. Therefore, *intense* is a synonymous term with *vivid*. *Tedious* means boring or dull, which is very different from the definition of *vivid*. *Suave* is an adjective that is used to describe people and their behaviors and is therefore not synonymous with *vivid*, which is used to describe the sensory experience of something. *Maddening* is an adjective that means annoying or infuriating. *Generic* refers to members of a whole group of similar things, which has nothing to do with *vivid*.

2. E: *Pedestrian* is a noun that means a person who goes or travels on foot. *Conductor, driver,* and *pilot* are all nouns that describe individuals operating or controlling a form of transportation, and by their nature are not *pedestrians*. An *automobile* is a vehicle and not a *pedestrian*. Therefore, the synonymous term is *walker*, which similarly can be defined as a person that walks.

3. D: *Aroma* is a noun that means an odor or fragrance, especially an agreeable or pleasant one. *Odor*, then, is the synonymous term. *Distant* and *distinct* are both adjectives that refer to an object's positioning in relation to some other object or concept. *Horror*, like *aroma*, is a noun describing a sensory experience, but *horror* is associated with terror and fear rather than pleasantness. *Sound* is another sense word, but it is not a synonym of *aroma*.

4. C: *Legendary* is an adjective meaning of or relating to a legend and is specifically associated with stories that are nonhistorical or fantastical in one way or another. *Anonymous* is an adjective that refers to someone being unknown and is not directly related to *legendary*. *Typical* is an adjective that can be defined as conforming to a particular type and is used synonymously with terms like normal and average. Therefore, *typical* and *legendary* have nearly opposite meanings. *Cynical* and *judicial* are both adjectives that can be used to describe a person's mindset or beliefs and are not specifically related to the concept of legend in any way. *Mythical* is an adjective meaning pertaining to or involving a myth. Since myth and legend are essentially synonymous terms, *mythical* is accordingly synonymous with *legendary*.

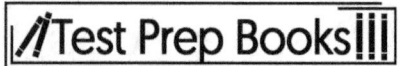

Answer Explanations

5. E: *Ruin* is a verb meaning to bring or reduce to a diminished or decayed state. *Idolize* is a verb meaning to worship as a god and so is somewhat contradictory to the idea of ruining something. *Build, transform,* and *reconstruct* refer to the alteration of something but in none of these terms is there the idea that the thing being altered is being made worse or being diminished. *Destroy* is a verb meaning, among other things, to reduce to a useless form and to render ineffective. Therefore, *destroy* is the synonymous term.

6. B: *Manufacture* is a verb meaning to make by hand or machinery and is usually associated with the making of something on a large scale. *Disrupt* is a verb that means to cause disorder or even to destroy and so is somewhat contrary to the meaning of *manufacture*. *Recognize* is a verb that involves the memory of another person and is therefore more personal than the concept of manufacturing something. *Trigger* is a verb that means to cause or initiate something but does not refer to a specific process of creating something in the way *manufacture* does. To *count* is to number things, which is unrelated to *manufacture*. *Produce* is a verb that specifically refers to the process of creating or bringing something about. *Produce* is therefore synonymous with *manufacture*.

7. E: *Hoist* is a verb that means to raise or haul something up. *Attach* is a verb that means to join or to fasten and does not refer to the raising up of something. *Hamper* and *volunteer* are both verbs that refer to the effect one's actions may have or intend to have on another and similarly are not synonymous with *hoist*. *Lower* is an antonym of *hoist*, as it related to moving something down instead of up. The correct choice, therefore, is *lift*. *Lift* can be defined quite similarly to *hoist* as to raise or bring to a higher level.

8. C: *Banquet* is a noun that can be defined as a lavish meal, usually for ceremonial purposes. *Announcement, castle, rug,* and *silverware* are all nouns that may be associated with *banquet* due to the connection between ceremonial banquets and medieval kingdoms, but the terms themselves are not directly synonymous. *Feast*, on the other hand, is a noun meaning a rich or abundant meal, and is therefore the synonymous term to *banquet*.

9. B: *Industrious* is an adjective meaning working energetically and devotedly. *Adventurous* is an adjective meaning courageous or bold. While adventurous people may be industrious, the two terms do not have the same meaning. A person who is *resistant* is usually against something or unaccepting of change. This is unrelated to being a devoted worker. A student can be *smart,* displaying above average intelligence, without being *industrious*. *Lazy* is the opposite of *industrious*. *Hardworking*, which is an adjective synonymous with terms like conscientious, dedicated, and diligent, is therefore the synonymous term to *industrious*.

10. E: *Vacant* is an adjective meaning unoccupied or deserted. *Related*, an adjective meaning connected to something else, does not have any connection to *vacant*. *Implied* is an adjective meaning hidden or unspoken, and something being hidden is clearly not the same as something being deserted. Similarly, *missing* is an adjective that implies something is gone that once was there, whereas in the term *vacant*, all that is implied is that the object itself is unoccupied or deserted. *Unsure* is an adjective that typically refers to a state of mind and not a physical object or place, and therefore is not synonymous with *vacant*. *Empty*, however, is an adjective that means containing nothing, and is therefore directly synonymous with *vacant*.

11. A: *Outskirts* is a noun that refers to the outer or bordering areas of a city or other large settlement of people. *Reservoir* is a noun that refers to any place where a large amount of something is gathered or held and does not refer to any sort of human settlement. Therefore, the two terms are not synonymous.

Answer Explanations

Metropolis is a noun that can be defined as any large and busy city. The idea of a *metropolis* is therefore somewhat opposite to the idea of *outskirts*, which must exist away from the city itself. Similarly, *central* is related to the middle of something as opposed to its outer limits. *Boundary* is a noun that generally refers to anything that indicates or defines the limits of something and is therefore synonymous with *outskirts*.

12. C: *Seldom* is an adverb that can be defined as not often or infrequent. Therefore, it is directly synonymous with *rarely*, which similarly can be defined as hardly ever or infrequently, and it is directly antonymous to *often*. *Conventional*, *egotistical*, and *sleepy* are all adjectives, and therefore cannot be synonymous with an adverb like *seldom*. Additionally, the term *conventional* refers to something ordinary or commonplace, and therefore would not have the same meaning as seldom.

13. A: *Thrifty* is an adjective that is synonymous with terms like frugal and prudent. *Sneaky* is an adjective that is synonymous with terms like dishonest and devious, and therefore it has much more negative connotations than *thrifty*. *Practical* and *pleasant*, on the other hand, are both adjectives with much more positive connotations, but neither has the exact same meaning as *thrifty*. *Practical* is defined as useful or constructive, while *pleasant* means friendly or polite. *Likely* means probable, and is unrelated to *thrifty*. *Economical*, on the other hand, is directly synonymous with *thrifty* since the term *economical* is defined as thrifty or frugal management.

14. D: *Flimsy* is an adjective meaning not strong, as well as light and thin. Therefore, it is directly synonymous with *thin*. *Amusing* is an adjective synonymous with terms like entertaining or diverting, and therefore has more positive connotations than something being *flimsy*. The adjective *convenient* similarly has positive connotations, with it being synonymous to terms like *favorable* and *good*. *Rowdy* is an adjective that refers to a noisy or disorderly disposition, and therefore is not commonly associated with the idea of something being weak or light. Something that is *solid* would be the opposite of flimsy.

15. C: *Coax* is a verb that means to attempt to influence, usually by flattery. *Despise*, *harm*, and *trouble* are all verbs that have negative connotations, usually involving the infliction of some discomfort or distress to the receiving party of the action. Therefore, they are not synonymous with *coax*, which has a much gentler connotation. *Advance*, meaning to move forward, has no direct connection to *coax*. *Persuade* is a verb with a similar connotation to *coax*, with it being defined as to induce to believe. Therefore, *persuade* and *coax* are synonymous.

Analogies

16. A: This is an object/function analogy. One uses a *pot* to *boil*. Likewise, one uses a *rope* to *climb*. A *faucet* is not an action, so even though *water* comes out of one, it is not the correct completion to the analogy. Similarly, a *mirror* provides a *reflection*, but since *reflection* is a noun, it cannot be the correct answer choice. A *chef* is the person, not the object, who *cooks*. *Temper* is also not an object; therefore, even though it is associated with *rage*, it is not the correct answer.

17. E: This is a category/type analogy. *Hydrogen* is a specific type of *element*, just as *calico* is a type of *cat*. Canine is a type of species, but the relationship is presented in the wrong order. None of the other answer choices represent words that have a category/type relationship.

18. C: This is a degree of intensity analogy. *Miniscule* is an extreme version of *small*, while *ailing* is an extreme version of *unhealthy*. *Chagrin* and *elusive* do not have a meaningful relationship, nor do

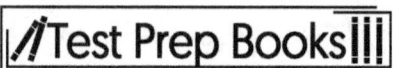

confined and *rotten*. *Tall* is the opposite of *short*, and *cough* may be associated with *allergy*, but it does not represent a lesser degree.

19. E: This is a part/whole analogy. This analogy focuses on natural formations and their highest points. The peak of a mountain is its highest point, just as the crest is the highest rise in a wave.

20. C: This is a part/whole analogy. Flour is an ingredient of cake, just as yeast is an ingredient of bread. Spoons and ovens are instruments that are typically associated with soup and casseroles, but they are not ingredients. Lettuce is an ingredient of salad, but the relationship is presented in the wrong order. Hot fudge is a topping, not an ingredient, of ice cream.

21. B: This is a synonym analogy. *Grief* and *sadness* mean the same thing, as do *merriment* and *happiness*. Though a birthday is a cause for celebration, the two words are not synonymous. *Vexation* means anger, while *reconciliation* typically refers to bringing together that which was previously separated. Tears are a manifestation of the action of crying. Joy is a type of emotion, but the words are not synonymous since there are many emotions other than joy.

22. E: This is a user/instrument analogy. A doctor uses a stethoscope, and a carpenter uses a hammer. *Teachers* use *books*, and *plumbers* work with *pipes*, but these relationships are not presented in the correct order. *Nurses* and *sculptors* may be associated with *hospitals* and *museums*, but those are not instruments.

23. A: This is a category/type analogy. Green is a type of color, just as mammals are a type of animal. A dog is a type of mammal, but the relationship is presented in the wrong order. *Purple* and *violet* are synonymous. Appliances are not a type of kitchen; they are found in the kitchen. The color spectrum is represented on the rainbow, but it is not a type of rainbow.

24. B: This is an object/function analogy. A pencil's function is to write, and soap's function is to cleanse. The remaining words may be commonly associated with soap, but they do not represent its primary purpose.

25. C: This is a category/type relationship. Golden Retriever is a breed of dog, and American Quarter Horse is a breed of horse. A dolphin is a mammal, not a fish. Siamese is a type of cat, but the relationship is presented in the wrong order. A cobra is a type of snake, but the relationship is presented in the wrong order. A child is a young human, not a breed of human.

26. E: This is an object/function analogy. The function of brakes is to stop an object in motion, and the purpose of money is to purchase goods and services. While food does hydrate, its primary purpose is to nourish, and most living creatures need water to fully hydrate themselves. *Promise* and *pledge* have a synonymous relationship, as do *tape* and *adhesive*. Deer can be hunted, but that is not their primary function.

27. A: This is a symbol/representation analogy. Love is often represented by the color red (e.g., hearts). Similarly, royalty has historically been symbolized by the color purple. A crown or scepter might represent royalty as well, but the relationship in this analogy is between a color and what it symbolizes. Gold and silver might be associated with royalty because they typically represent wealth, but they are not the primary colors that have historically represented royalty.

Answer Explanations

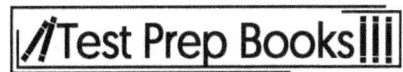

28. D: This is a grammatical analogy. *Pair* and *pear* are homonyms, which mean that they are pronounced the same way but are spelled differently and have different meanings. *Stair* and *stare* are also homonyms.

29. C: This is a degree of intensity analogy. *Famished* means extremely hungry, and *irate* means extremely angry. Upset, irritated, and annoyed indicate a lesser degree of anger. *Hatred* can indicate extreme anger, but it is not the correct answer for this analogy because it is a noun, not an adjective.

30. E: This is a part to whole analogy. Many *chapters* make up a *novel*, in the same way that many *brushstrokes* make up a *painting*.

Reading Section

1. D: Choice *D* matches the way Laura feels about the shoes sitting unused in the closet. There is no physical description of the shoes to indicate if Choice *A* is accurate or not. Choices *B* and *E* describe actions that are not mentioned in the passage. Choice *C* is the opposite of how Laura feels about the shoes sitting in the closet.

2. C: The passage's narration suggests that this punishment is unfair using Laura's logic on the matter. The passage does not make clear if Johnny was ever punished, so Choice *A* is incorrect. Laura is no longer pleased about anything after having gotten caught, so Choice *B* is incorrect. The passage makes it clear that Laura hates being small, so Choice *D* is also incorrect. The revenge plan in Choice *E* is never brought up in the passage.

3. E: The passage says that Laura couldn't balance in the shoes; she decided to put them back since she knew she couldn't safely wear them. While she would have put the shoes back where she got them, her main reason for doing so was that she couldn't balance in them, so Choice *A* is not the best answer. All of the other choices don't fit with anything the passage says.

4. B: The passage's main point is to get across the idea that this responsibility should not be taken lightly. Choice *A* is incorrect because the passage does not focus on how adorable puppies are. Choice *E* is something the passage says but not its main idea. Choice *C* is incorrect because, while the passage assumes most people "likely already know" this, it does not indicate that everyone knows it, and this is not the main focus of the passage. Choice *D* makes an assumption the passage does not support.

5. C: Choice *C* is correct, as it is the only option not included in the passage. All of the other options are included (Choice *A*: "A puppy has no idea that it's done something wrong if it isn't taught by its owner ... it's only a baby"; Choice *B*: "It is an animal, after all"; Choice *D*: "it will also need training and discipline"; Choice *E*: "As the person responsible for your new dog's well-being, you must be able to handle these things").

6. D: The passage emphasizes the importance of proper training for dogs. Choices *A* and *B* are not mentioned in the passage. Choices *C* and *E* give very specific advice that the passage does not mention, and its main idea is not about feeding or walking a dog.

7. C: The passage is focused on the responsibility of pet owners to train their dogs. Choice *A* may be true but would not explain the emphasis on proper training. Choice *B* is incorrect because the author does not express anger or a belief that no one is raising their puppies right. Choices *D* and *E* are incorrect

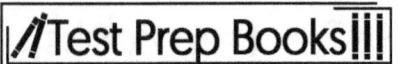

Answer Explanations

because the author does not express hatred or fear of dogs; rather, the passage suggests the author cares about dogs and wants people to raise them well.

8. E: The passage specifically mentions that Grayson is willing to share his favorite food with Ellie, and the passage then describes how he feels about parting with his fruit snacks. Choice *A* is incorrect, as the passage suggests grape is only one of multiple fruit snack flavors. Choice *B* is a fact about the fruit snacks but doesn't make them special. Choices *C* and *D* are not things the passage indicates.

9. A: Choice *A* matches what the passage says about Grayson even sharing his favorite food with the sister of his very good friend Vanessa. Choice *B* is incorrect; Vanessa was Grayson's friend, and Ellie is only described as her sister. Choices *C* and *D* are incorrect because they assume things about Ellie the passage does not indicate, and Choice *E* does the same with Vanessa.

10. B: Choice *B* is correct because it is an action Grayson can take to try to repair the broken friendships. Choice *A* assumes a teacher was not outside, which the passage does not indicate, and it is not clear how the teacher being outside would help them be friends again. Choice *C* is incorrect because there is no indication that the sisters are not nice people; it is reasonable for them to be upset about the rock hitting Ellie. The two would likely still be upset with Grayson if he threw the dirt clod in Choice *D*. Choice *E* would not be helpful and may even make them more upset with Grayson.

11. D: Choice *D* fits with the passage's lack of description of what Tim Winston was thinking. Choice *A* is not something reasonable to assume just because only his last name is given in the passage. The passage does not mention Tim before the shove, making Choice *B* incorrect. Choices *C* and *D* are not mentioned in the passage.

12. C: Choice *C* makes sense with the measurement of four years. Choices *A*, *D*, and *E* are objects not measured in years. Choice *B* is a different definition of the word *term* that does not work with the way it is used in the passage.

13. A: Choice *A* would likely bother him the most based on what the passage says about Washington disliking political parties. Choices *B* and *D* assume that he would be very specific about the length of time he thinks is fair to hold power, and the passage does not say this. The passage does not give a reason to believe he longed to be remembered, as in Choice *C*, nor does it give a reason to believe that he would be unhappy with the presidency living on, as in Choice *E*.

14. B: The passage says that Washington did not want to hold this power for too long. Choices *A*, *C*, and *E* make assumptions about his feelings that are not supported by the passage. Choice *D* is incorrect because the passage does not indicate that the political party system had anything to do with how long he stayed in office.

15. A: The passage states directly that Washington did not like political parties. Choice *B* is something he may have feared but not something the passage states as fact. Choice *C* is a story people tell about George Washington that is not mentioned in the passage. Choice *D* is not true of all presidents; the passage only states that Washington served two four-year terms. Choice *E* is incorrect because the passage gives no indication that Washington hated being president.

16. A: The passage discusses recent technological advances in cars and suggests that this trend will continue in the future with self-driving cars. Choice *B* and *C* are not true, so these are both incorrect.

Answer Explanations

Choice D is also incorrect because the passage suggests continuing growth in technology, not a peak. Choice E is not shown in the passage, as it states that self-driving cars are on the horizon.

17. B: The pairing of the statement regarding research money with the author's suggestion that humanities face an uphill battle suggests a connection between the two. In other words, humanities do not bring in the kind of funding that science, technology, engineering, and mathematics (STEM) subjects and research do. As a result, universities don't fund them the same way. Choice A is incorrect because there is no indication that this is true. Choice C is incorrect because although it might solve the problem, that solution is not the focus of this passage. Choice D is incorrect because while there is an implication that STEM receives more money, money is not the only valuable aspect of education or universities. Choice E is incorrect because it is an extreme position not directly supported by the passage.

18. C: If predators rely on prey for food and nutrition and if cats are predators of mice, then cats rely on mice for food and nutrition. Choice A is incorrect. The prey is eaten by the predator. Choice C is incorrect. The prey (the mice) are the ones who develop the feature that allow them to escape from the predators (the cats). Choice D is incorrect. *Extinct relationship* is not an actual term. The term used in the passage is *distinct relationship*.

19. C: The sentence clearly states that they tend to crowd out native species. Choice A is incorrect because it is the opposite of what invasive species do. Choice B is incorrect because symbiotic relationships require coexistence, and crowding out is not coexistence. Choice D is incorrect because invasive species can often find a way to thrive, as demonstrated by the example of the Everglades pythons. Choice E is incorrect because invasive species use up or deplete the resources that native species need.

20. E: The overall subject of the sentence is keeping the costs of home improvement down, with suggestions for doing so listed. Choices A, B, C, and D are incorrect. These refer to the ways to keep costs down, but independently, none of these are the subject of the full sentence.

21. D: The passage ends by stating that production did not decline until the 1970s, so Choice D is correct. If production did not decline until the 1970s, then it could not have declined one hundred years ago. Therefore, Choice A in incorrect. Evidence was presented that asbestos was dangerous early on, and asbestos was produced for over one hundred years, so it can be reasoned that the evidence was around long before the decline in production during the 1970s. This means that Choice B is incorrect. The passage does not state that the durability of asbestos ever declined, so Choice C is incorrect. The 1970s were not within the last ten years, so Choice E is incorrect.

22. E: The passage states that the main asteroids that lie in a tight belt between Mars and Jupiter are theorized to be fragments of a planet that was forming but broke into pieces due to a collision. Choice A is incorrect. These are thought to have been created from a giant cloud of gas and dust. Choice B is incorrect. Mars and Jupiter are the planets that have a tight belt of asteroids between them. Choice C is incorrect because Earth was not the theorized result. Choice D is incorrect. Comets are thought to be remnants from that giant cloud of gas and dust that created the Sun, planets, and moons.

23. D: The main point of this passage is to define osteoporosis. Choice A is incorrect because the passage does not list ways that people contract osteoporosis. Choice B is incorrect because the passage does not mention any treatment options. While the passage does briefly mention prevention, it does not explain how, so Choice C is incorrect. Choice E is incorrect because the passage is not about the function of bones in general, but specifically about osteoporosis.

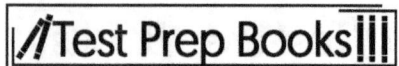

Answer Explanations

24. C: Choice *C* is correct because there are not enough details in the passage to determine the answer to this question. There is no mention of his performance after half of his tutoring sessions or after his last session, so Choices *A* and *B* are incorrect. It might be tempting to guess that he showed improvement after the last session since his ability to pass was unclear after several sessions but he was able to pass during the last week of class. However, the question asks us to determine when he began to show improvement. There is no indication that his last tutoring session had already occurred. Choice *D* is incorrect. Jason did buckle down during the last week of class and ended up passing, but we do not know if he had already shown some improvement before the last week of class.

25. B: The passage asks how many know about this after saying that most know the previous facts, implying that people are not as likely to know about this system. Choices *A* and *C* are a higher level of knowledge than the passage implies is accurate. Choices *D* and *E* are incorrect because, while the passage suggests that most people don't know about the Minor League class system, it does not suggests that no one, or no one aside from baseball players, knows anything at all about the Minor League.

26. E: Single-A players do receive more pay than Rookies, since the passage states that Rookies receive the least pay. All other choices give relationships that are the opposite of what the passage states.

27. C: The first sentence of the passage states that if a player is being paid, that person is playing professionally. Choice *A* suggests this is not the case, which is incorrect. Choice *B* is incorrect because all classes, not just those above Class A Short Season, have professional players. Choice *D* is incorrect because players in all the classes are paid. Choice *E* is incorrect because the passage does not suggest that there are differing views on who is professional or that the year has anything to do with it.

28. A: The levels are called classes in the passage. Choices *B* and *C* are different ways of saying *level* that the passage does not use. Choices *D* and *E* are other words associated with baseball but not the levels of the Minor League system.

Dear SSAT Elementary Level Test Taker,

Thank you for purchasing this study guide for your SSAT Elementary Level exam. We hope that we exceeded your expectations.

Our goal in creating this study guide was to cover all of the topics that you will see on the test. We also strove to make our practice questions as similar as possible to what you will encounter on test day. With that being said, if you found something that you feel was not up to your standards, please send us an email and let us know.

We would also like to let you know about other books in our catalog that may interest you.

SSAT Middle Level

This can be found on Amazon: amazon.com/dp/1637759835

ISEE Lower Level

amazon.com/dp/1637754132

We have study guides in a wide variety of fields. If the one you are looking for isn't listed above, then try searching for it on Amazon or send us an email.

Thanks Again and Happy Testing!
Product Development Team
support@testprepbooks.com

Online Resources

Included with your purchase are multiple online resources. This includes the practice tests in an interactive format and a convenient study timer to help you manage your time.

Scan the QR code or go to this link to access this content:

testprepbooks.com/online387/ssat-elem

The first time you access the page, you will need to register as a "new user" and verify your email address.

If you have any issues, please email support@testprepbooks.com.

Thank you for letting us be a part of your studying journey!

www.ingramcontent.com/pod-product-compliance
Lightning Source LLC
Chambersburg PA
CBHW080735230426
43665CB00020B/2749